SEASONS and SELF

"My religion is nature.
That's what arouses those feelings of wonder
and mysticism and gratitude in me."

(Oliver Sacks)

Other Publications by Rex A. E. Hunt

New Green Shoots and Other Story Sermons
(1993, Joint Board of Christian Education)

* **When Progressives Gather Together:
Liturgy, Lectionary, Landscape… And Other Explorations**
(2016, Morning Star Publishing)

* **Cards, Carols, and Claus:
Christmas in Popular Culture and Progressive Christianity**
(2013, Morning Star Publishing)

* **Against the Stream:
Progressive Christianity Between Pulpit and Pew**
(2012, Morning Star Publishing)

(Editor and Contributor) with John W. H. Smith)
**Why Weren't We Told?
A Handbook on 'progressive' Christianity**
(2012, Polebridge Press)

* **New Life. Rediscovering Faith:
Stories from Progressive Christians**
(2013, Morning Star Publishing)

(Editor and Contributor) with Gregory C. Jenks)
* **Wisdom and Imagination:
Religious Progressives and the Search for Meaning**
(2014, Morning Star Publishing)

* *Also available in USA through Wipf & Stock*

DISCOURSES
ON BEING 'AT HOME'
IN NATURE

SEASONS & SELF

REX A. E. HUNT

WITH ELEVEN ORIGINAL POEMS BY JOHN CRANMER

COVENTRY
PRESS

Published in Australia by
Coventry Press
33 Scoresby Road
Bayswater Vic 3153

ISBN: 9780648230328

© Rex A. E. Hunt 2018

All rights reserved. Other than for and subject to the conditions prescribed under the *Copyright Act*, no part of this publication may be reproduced, stored in a retrieval system, or transmitted in any form or by any means, electronic, mechanical, photocopying, recording or otherwise, without the prior written permission of the publisher.

First published in 2018

Cataloguing-in-Publication entry is available for the National Library of Australia
http:/catalogue.nla.gov.au/

Every effort has been made to trace copyright holders and to obtain their permission for the use of copyright material.

The author and publisher apologise for any errors or omissions and would be grateful if notified of any corrections and acknowledgments that should be incorporated in future reprints or editions of this book.

Text design by Filmshot Graphics (FSG)
Cover design by Ian James – www.jgd.com.au

Printed in Australia

CONTENTS

Introduction 11

Prologue 17
To Walk on Green Earth!
Religious Naturalism and Ritual in Progressive Spirituality

Addresses/Sermons

No. 1

Seasons and Self 41
Theme focus: Seasons
Poem: "Winter is Broken!!"

No. 2

Celebrating Earth and Wonder in Early Spring 53
Theme focus: Earth/Early Spring
Poem: "And the Coming of Spring"

No. 3

Religion and the Need for Humour in our Lives 62
Theme focus: Humour

No. 4

'Environment' is More Than our Sun, Sand and Surf 71
Theme focus: Environment Day/Climate Change

No 5

Learning to be More Genuinely Human 82
Theme focus: Wisdom/Imagination

No. 6

Autumn: The Season of Leaves and Harvest 93
Theme: Autumn in the Southern Hemisphere
Poem: "Exploring a Quietness of Trees"

No. 7
Some Stuff I Have Picked Up Along the Way About Jesus and G-o-d and the World 102
Theme focus: G-o-d/Jesus

No. 8
Of Dogs and Cats and…: Towards a Life-Centered Religion 111
Theme focus: Blessing of Animals
Poem: "Missie"

No 9
The Liberation and Novelty of 'Evolutionary' Life 119
Theme focus: Evolution/Darwin
Poem: "Shaping the Marrow of Every Stone"

No. 10
Mate, the Desert is G-o-d's own Country 130
Theme focus: Desert/Wilderness
Poem: "ReWilding Suburbia"

No. 11
Advent: The Sacred in the Ordinary and Symbolic 141
Theme focus: Advent/Ordinary
Poem: "Blackbirds at First Light"

No. 12
When Religious People can be Down-right Silly! 149
Theme focus: Apocalyptic/End Times

No. 13
The Earth that we Knew, is Gone… Long Live Eaarth! 154
Theme focus: Ocean
Poem: "Thunder Cave"

No. 14
As We Live in the Unseen G-o-d/Creativity 165
Theme focus: After Christmas/Year's end

No. 15

Coming Home to the Cosmos 172
Theme: Cosmos
Poem: "Planet and Self Entwined"

No. 16

Challenging the Status Quo and Inhumanities 181
Theme focus: Family

No. 17

An Indigenous Gift: Living with the Land 191
Theme focus: Land/Power
Poem: "Lost Mantras for Gondwana"

No. 18

Immersed in the Mysteries of 'Creation' 203
Theme focus: Creation/Universe

No. 19

Children: The Genesis of Hope 210
Theme focus: Children/Education
Poem: "Will's Tadpole Sanctuary"

No. 20

A Nod and a Wink, and Maybe 'Life-Enhancing' 219
Theme focus: Meaning

No. 21

The Challenge of Extravagance and Celebration 226
Theme focus: Celebration/Life

No. 22

Of Evolution and G-o-d, and the Unfolding Interconnectedness of Life 232
Theme focus: Evolution

No. 23
Slow Food Not Fast Food: We Are What We Eat 242
Theme focus: Food/Eating

Postlude 250

Combined Bibliography 252

About the Author 263

About the Poet 264

To
*All those who continue to push
religious and theological boundaries
and commit themselves wholeheartedly to life*

And in memory of Harry T. Cook
*American Episcopal Priest,
who died 9 October 2017*

"Conserve Earth, her atmosphere, her waterways and seas, her land, her creatures as good stewards would estates entrusted to their care and protection.
One can lick away on an ice cream cone only so long before it disappears."
(Published in the last paragraph of Cook's final Internet column, titled 'Testament')

Acknowledgments

• An earlier version of the sermon/address *'The Earth That We Knew Is Gone: Long, Live Eaarth!'* has appeared in **Against the Stream: Progressive Christianity Between Pulpit and Pew** (Morning Star Publishing, 2013).

• An earlier version of the sermon/address *'Coming Home To The Cosmos'* has appeared in **Against the Stream: Progressive Christianity Between Pulpit and Pew** (Morning Star Publishing, 2013).

• An earlier version of the sermon/address *'Environment Is More Than Our Sun, Sand, And Surf'* has appeared in **When Progressives Gather Together: Liturgy, Lectionary, Landscape… And Other Explorations** (Morning Star Publishing, 2016).

•An earlier version of the sermon/address *'Of Evolution and G-o-d, and the Unfolding Interconnectedness of Life'* has appeared in **When Progressives Gather Together: Liturgy, Lectionary, Landscape… And Other Explorations** (Morning Star Publishing, 2016).

• The eleven poems by **John Cranmer** are published with the permission of the poet.

INTRODUCTION

> "Whether we continue to talk about God is not so important
> as whether we retain the sense of wonder
> which keeps us aware that ours is a holy place."
> *(Sam Keen)*

Once again, I have been prodded into putting 'pen to paper' to share some of my thoughts and interests as they were given life in Addresses, Presentations and Sermons over the past few years.

This particular collection reflects a major slab of my latter-stage thinking. Some have been presented as sermons in congregations – mainline/oldline and Unitarian–but many have come to life in other situations – keynote presentations, panel discussions, and small study groups. Four have appeared as sermons in two of my earlier books, but have been revised or updated. All have had an oral beginning, sometimes just after dawn broke. And sometimes after I have done a dose of unlearning before committing my thoughts to paper, and before opening my mouth!

Brazilian Rubem Alves (1933-2014) – theologian, philosopher, poet, psychoanalyst, and one of the founders of liberation theology – has been an inspiration for my oral/writing process. "I am not after conclusions", he said, and then wrote, "Conclusions are meant to shut... Every conclusion brings the thought process to a halt." *(Alves 1990:9)* As I have suggested in another place, in my preaching/presentation style I try to invite others to both get curious and excited about what they hear, and to explore further – beyond the tyranny of clear and distinct ideas! If that happens then I feel I have been faithful to my calling as a communicator, as well as being respectful of my hearer as she comes to her own conclusions.

So what is offered in this collection, as they were when they had a sound-full life, are about 'likelihoods', and being 'open-ended' rather than closing down any discussion with persuasion by argument. They are not organised to follow an exegetical preaching pattern common with many preachers. Instead, each presentation has been shaped into several short cameos – hopefully moving horizontally like a map, rather than vertically like an office building. The intent is to strike a chord rather than 'shoehorning' something – ideas, answers, doctrine, correct belief – into people, even when I challenge the parochial and limited claims of traditional religions, or so-called pious biblical argument based on a proof-text zeal. As in my other collection, *Against the Stream*, some touch on similar issues which can create areas of repetition.

The title... **Seasons and Self.** I am a self-professed religious naturalist, progressive liturgist, and social ecologist. That puts me squarely within a post-liberal/ 'progressive' orientation. It also means I do not see myself as having to believe in the god G-o-d, although when that term is used by religious naturalists it is more often than not used naturalistically.[1] So a little more about religious naturalism (RN) and 'progressive' because you will encounter this thought in several of the chapters...

The capacity of the natural world to inspire a religious response from humans has long been recognised. The book's **Prologue** goes into the religious naturalism (RN) orientation in more detail, but briefly, RN is a life of contemplation, inquiry, and moral practice devoted to the beauty and creativity of nature. An integration of science and religion. It is not a religion. It is a *religious orientation*. It holds that the natural universe is all there is – that there is religious meaning and value in nature. The *super*natural does not exist, so no gods, spirits, souls, or miracles.

As naturalism, it seeks knowledge about the universe right here in this world of matter and energy, which includes our minds, our beliefs and whatever else the world of the supernatural tries to encompass. As religious, it seeks to frame our experience in a field of meaning and purpose by encouraging feelings of awe, mystery and gratitude, and promoting an ongoing discipline of reflection, contemplation and celebration. It does not refer to any particular faith tradition.

---

[1] Stone: "Of course you can still ask why use the term God, since it is so confusing and has such oppressive baggage. However [writers such as Wieman, Peters, Kaufman] address that term and insist that it is a powerful word that we cannot get along without, at least in Western culture." (Stone 2008, as recorded by Susan Barreto, on RNA web site.)

A forerunner of modern religious naturalism (RN) is Baruch Spinoza (1632-1677), who used the phrase 'God or nature' in Book 1 of his *Ethics*. But it would be remiss of me not to also jump ahead two hundred years and name another – Australian born Samuel Alexander (1859-1938) who spent all of his teaching career at Manchester University in England, and who was an important influence on some streams within early RN thinking.

My initial attraction to RN was via liberal/process theology scholars such as Henry Nelson Wieman, Bernard Meland – 1940s theologians at the University of Chicago – and then from the 1970s, Karl Peters. Some years later I added Gordon Kaufman to my list. All sought to 'reconstruct' traditional Christian theism. Taking just one example... Meland, in his 1934 book, **Modern Man's Worship**, was ahead of his theological time when he suggested: 'What we need is to... understand in our very bones that even in our spiritual behaviour we are an expression of earth forces. We are the universe come to consciousness.'

Those in the current RN 'big tent' who now excite my interest are Loyal Rue, Jerome Stone, and author and cell biologist, Ursula Goodenough – who engage the religious turn from 'tradition' towards 'heresy' (another opinion), a shift in focus from transcendence to 'horizontal immanence', and post-traditionalism, often in very deliberate and provocative ways. To echo sociologist Peter Berger: the heretical turn is an important task in contemporary religious studies. To echo Karl Marx: what is the human quest about, to understand the world or to change it?

And now 'progressive'... Here 'progressive' is a short-hand way of saying progressive religion, primarily shaped by a critical understanding of the Galilean sage called Yeshu'a/Jesus, coupled with just a hint of 'Engaged Buddhism' as expressed by Thich Nhat Hạnh.[2]

Much of my professional life has been spent with the 'historical'/ human Jesus rather than the 'mythical' Christ of faith. The former is about a human being crucified by the Romans as a state criminal. The latter is about Jesus as God incarnate, begotten of the Father, born of a virgin... The difficulty is nothing comes directly from Jesus. Not only

---

[2] See the chapter on 'Wisdom'.

did he not write anything, what we do have – called Gospels – is what others wrote about him or believed about him. None of those writings occurred during the lifetime of Jesus. They are not verbatim records of what Jesus said.

Australian biblical scholar Gregory Jenks highlighted this difference in his cameo entry in our book ***Why Weren't We Told?*** He pointed out that the issue is the tension between what a historian can say about Jesus and what Christianity says about Jesus.

> The gap between the "Jesus of history" and the "Christ of faith" has been at the centre of a major and continuing controversy. At the heart of this controversy is the question of truth; not simply what is true, but who determines what is true? Is the truth about Jesus settled by the church's traditional creeds, or is the truth about Jesus something that might yet be clarified by new research that is independent of – and not in any sense controlled by – the Church?
> *(Jenks 2013:39-40)*

Those who seek to follow the historical Jesus are not trying to determine precisely what Jesus said "but to recognise the style or voiceprint of the teaching." *(Galston 2012:47)* Such research explorations are reflected in the following chapters.

To the book… When you open the following pages you will find each chapter has a themed focus, reflecting in part what is to come, as well as echoed in the collection title. A theme can be free-flowing and is much wider than a text. Hopefully together they – book title and chapter focus – might at least be fragments of insight. But again, following Alves, what matters in the long run is "not what I say but the words that you hear, coming out of your forgotten depths." *(Alves 1990:18)* As I have learned: there are pockets of meaning that sometimes we can enlarge. It can sometimes transform one's life. So, as another has said, 'have faith in a seed'.

My thanks… To several people. To colleagues here and overseas who tap into my web site each week to explore my offerings, and are generous enough to offer words of thanks and encouragement; to those who have attended the various keynote presentations or sat through sermons in congregations, for their active listening and helpful discussion (and buying some of my books); to my spouse Dylis who is always loving and supportive; to my three grand children who are beginning to test poppy with their learning – even though they are only 6, 5, and 4 years respectively; and to the other eleven (11) blokes who, together with me, comprise the 'Coffee Club' – ordinary Aussie blokes who attempt to keep me grounded in the real world (although I still have a secret or three up my sleeve!) as we support and enjoy each other's company of a Tuesday morning at a local coffee shop, and attempt to solve the problems of the self, the world – and the local Men's Lawn Bowling Club!

My professional thanks must also go to the many authors whose thoughts I have discovered and been stimulated by. As readers, I encourage you to seek out their published works, especially as detailed in the Combined Bibliography. Yes, all of them in all their variety.

But I must say a special word about two poets. Max Coots' (1927-2009) reflections "of common things" in his 46 year old 'first' book, **Seasons of the Self**.[3] I bought it way back when it was first released, and despite all the house shifts over that same period of time, I have kept it on my library shelves, and read its contents often. I knew little more about the author except what the publisher chose to place on the back-cover flap: "A man of diverse interests, he is active in various professions – as writer, as [Unitarian-Universalist] minister, and as a college professor" - where he taught 'Contemporary Social Problems' at Clarkson College. Much later, thanks to the internet, I was able to update myself further on his writings - and sculptures. My continuing appreciation for his poetic thoughts are expressed in the adopted title of this book.

The second poet I wish to thank is my Australian colleague John Cranmer. He has an uncanny ability to take both the ordinary and the sacred within the Australian landscape, especially places of intense presence, and give them new life through his verse. Having worked with him on another writing project, I consider it an honour to be given permission to publish some of his poetic responses to my thoughts and writings contained in this book. They are all the better for his contributions.

---

[3] Coots published two other books: **View from a Tree** (1989) and **Leaning Against the Wind: A Selection of Sermons** (1992).

And on the practical side… My thanks to Gwen and Laurie Mitchell, and to Dylis McConnell-Hunt for proof-reading the text, to Michael Morwood and Noel Preston who were gracious enough to offer some words of encouragement and commendation, and to Hugh McGinlay, my publishing editor since 1993 - but now with the new publishing house, Coventry Press.

Finally, I continue to express my appreciation to those in Theological Seminary/United Faculty of Theology who encouraged me to think theologically and push boundaries, starting many moons ago! As I declared in *Against the Stream*, I always saw myself as an enthusiastic student but one who was never content with the standard theological diet served up at the College. The then academic staff, but especially my Project/Thesis supervisor, Reverend Professor Harry Wardlaw, former Professor of Systematic Theology, offered an environment where it was safe to be exploratory and innovative rather than conservative and repeat the 'orthodox' past. My grateful thanks to all.

oo0oo

'If there is any sense to seasons it is this: that time is timeless and time is life'. We are all on the edge of time – right now. Being on the edge of time, we are always going into the future. It is an unknown future. Yet it is a future upon which our thinking and actions will make a difference. What kinds of new possibilities for existence are we being called to enable? What kind of story are we being called to live as we help create our future?

It is no longer 'real' for us to keep our eyes focused on anything but the realities of the world in which we live. Hosanna! Not in the highest, but right here. Right now. This.

> "This is an experimental universe. Our job is to create religious materials and let future generations find in them what is helpful."
> *(Stone, quoted by Susan Barreto)*

Rex A. E. Hunt
Spring 2017 Australia
Web site: www.rexaehuntprogressive.com

PROLOGUE

To Walk on Green Earth!
Religious Naturalism and Ritual in
Progressive Spirituality[4]

> "When I have a terrible need of - dare I say, 'religion'? - then
> I go outside at night and paint the stars."
> *(Vincent Van Gogh)*

> "I am a forty-two-year-old woman. I've never received a love letter,
> never received flowers from a man. I have attempted suicide and have
> contemplated it many times since.
> And yet these wonders I have known: a maple tree in autumn, each
> leaf exactly the colour of gold; a weed-like microcosm whose perfect
> petals are no bigger than the head of a pin.
> The dawning of each season with its own unique perfume, spring and
> autumn bringing the strongest scents.
> These and many other moments of grace have kept me going."
> *(Sam Keen)*

When a Pope bans it as at variance – 'wrong teaching' – with the stated beliefs or doctrines deemed as correct or orthodox, then there is a good chance you are on to something significant! That is what happened in 1864 when Pope Pius IX condemned religious naturalism[5] as 'heresy'

---

[4] An earlier draft was prepared for a 'Inspiring Earth Ethics' Conference.
[5] In January 1417, most likely in the library of the Benedictine Abbey of Fulda, Germany, Italian book hunter Poggio Bracciolini made the discovery of a lifetime. It was a manuscript of a book written almost 1500 years earlier—*De Rerum Natura* (On the Nature of Things) by Titus Lucretius Carus. This poetic, philosophical work was a key factor in enabling the Renaissance and reintroducing an empirically based, naturalistic view of the universe, which contributed to the rise to modern science. In his own time, around 50 BCE, Lucretius voiced in poetic form the essential teachings of the earlier Greek philosophers Democritus and Epicurus. With Poggio's fifteenth century discovery, a second, usually overlooked, wisdom tradition was revived as an alternative to the dominant Western religious tradition stemming from Plato and Aristotle." *(Karl Peters. Personal web site).* E. O. Wilson credits Thales, a philosopher who lived and worked in the Ancient Greek kingdom of Ionia in the 7th Century BCE, as the grandfather of naturalism.

in the first seven articles of the now infamous *Syllabus of Errors*. However, due to the current rise of progressive religious thought coupled with issues such as climate change and new insights about the nature of the universe, this new 'old' wisdom tradition, described by some advocates as the "forgotten alternative",[6] is awakening the imagination and social conscience of a growing number of people.

The thesis of this chapter is in two parts:

> (i) Contemporary religious naturalism with its trans- or post-traditional emphasis on religion and religiosity, where the issue of transcendence as supernatural is eclipsed by a more prominent concern with the immanent and natural boundaries of human meaning shaped by modern natural science, is a viable option to the dualism of traditional 'belief-centred' religious thinking. In short, in this the twenty-first century, religious naturalism is good heresy![7] But like participants in a wine appreciation course, to improve one's taste and discrimination of wine, budding religious naturalists need exposure, attention, understanding and a good book or teacher. *(Stone 2003:791)*

> (ii) Ritual provides us with a tool to think logically, emotionally and ecologically. During rituals "we have the experience, unique in our culture, of neither *opposing* nature or *trying* to be in communion with nature; but of finding ourselves within nature, and that is the key to sustainable culture."[8]

ooOoo

Religious Naturalism (RN) has been described by some advocates as the "forgotten alternative".

---

[6] Jerome Stone. *Religious Naturalism Today.*
[7] See "Introduction: What is Heresy?" by Paul Alan Laughlin, in R. Hunt & J. Smith (ed). *Why Weren't We Told?* In that collection, Laughlin describes 'heresy' in both its traditional sense ("...any belief, opinion, doctrine, or theory that is held by one or more proponents of a particular religion, but that is at variance with the beliefs or doctrines deemed as correct or orthodox") and also in a less loaded sense ("from the Greek *heterodoxos*, literally 'of other opinion'.") The latter suggests a more neutral sense of the term "than the more sinister, pejorative connotation it has had for most of Christian history and still in common parlance today".
[8] LcChapelle. "Ritual is Essential".

While it may be new to many, it has a long pedigree, stretching from Christian medieval times through to today where it has been preserved primarily within Unitarian spirituality and Religious Humanism. And centuries before all that when you take into consideration indigenous peoples nature-centric songlines or Dreaming stories that celebrate the sacred earth as the *Kunapipi*, 'earth mother'.

Religious naturalism, the religious orientation which is the matrix for this book, has two central aspects. One is an appreciation of religion with a view that nature can be a focus of religious attention.[9] The other is a naturalist view of how things happen in the world – in which the natural world is all there is, and that nothing other than natural may cause events in the world. Put more poetically:

> "For all we know and can know, what there is, and all there is, is the natural world."[10]

Let me broaden out these aspects.

Religious orientation includes *spiritual responses*, which can include feelings of appreciation, gratitude, humility, reverence, and joy at the wonder of being alive. It also includes *moral/ethical responses*, involving values rooted in nature – to seek justice and cooperation among social groups and balance in ecosystems.[11] Wonder, although not the only possible response when contemplating the immense scale of matter, space, and time, is surely appropriate once we realise we belong to something so very far beyond us. Such naturalistic wonder and awe counts as deeply spiritual.

Naturalist views, where "the scientific understanding of nature serves as the starting point, and its religious potential is then explored", *(Ursula Goodenough)* provide a framework for understanding what

---

[9] Definition: "...*religious* naturalism is that form of naturalism that can generally be defined as a deliberately *naturalistic engagement with religion and religiosity*." (Hogue 2010:85)
[10] Owen Flanagan, quoted in Hogue. *The Promise of Religious Naturalism*, 50.
[11] "The activism within religious naturalism... stems from the open this-worldliness of religious naturalism and the resultant view that 'redemption is not expected to happen to us; improvement is to be brought about by human activity'." (A comment on W. Drees "Thick Naturalism" by Hogue in *The Promise...*, 86)

seems real.[12] These include a central story – the Epic of Evolution[13] – that explains the origins of the cosmos and humans, with perspectives from which to consider why we do what we do. We are fully linked with our surroundings in time, space, matter/energy, and causality, and where the metaphor of 'web' is used to describe this interrelatedness[14] – we create the web and the web creates us. Within the relational web, we are also self-creative and thereby transform the web, for better or worse.[15]

> "As earth-creatures we do not live in straight lines; we truly do exist in a web, a network, a maze... When the relationality is mutually supportive, and not distorted, we truly can speak of 'mazing grace'." *(Larry Axel)*

Our very existence is rooted in the fundamental processes of the universe itself. "How can we not stand in awe before the fact of our emergence as a consequence of those same vast processes that created galaxies and suns and stars and planets?" *(David Bumbaugh)*

Professor of Theology Michael Hogue gathers up these characteristics and suggests, in part, that religious naturalism

> "...is a humble religious path that decentralizes the human species within the infinitely broader metaphysical and aesthetic rhythms of the Universe. It is a way of knowing that reveres the wisdom of collective human experience and reason more highly than any single sacred book or tradition. It is a quest for wisdom from wherever it may come: from the symbols, myths and rituals of the world's diverse religious traditions, from literature and the arts, from the intricate splendours of indigenous knowledges to the mind-bending ways of the modern sciences." *(Michael Hogue)*

---

[12] Goodenough calls this process *religiopoieisis*... the 'crafting of religion'.
[13] Also called "The Universe Story", "The Epic of Creation" and "The Evolutionary Epic".
[14] Some have challenged this understanding because the image of a web is too meagre and simple for the reality. A web is flat and finished 'and has the mortal frailty of the individual spider'. And although elastic it has insufficient depth
[15] Axel, R. C. "Meland and Loomer", 7

Religious naturalism does not require a belief in g-o-d although it may include belief in g-o-d naturalistically conceived.[16] For many religious naturalists the intellectual component of religious life takes the form of insight rather than specific beliefs. The 'naturalism' represented by current advocates[17] is diverse. Generally speaking they can be grouped as:

(i) those who think of g-o-d as the totality of the universe considered religiously;

(ii) those who conceive of g-o-d as the creative process within the universe;

(iii) those who think of g-o-d as the sum of human ideals, and

(iv) those who see no need to use the concept or terminology of g-o-d yet can still be called religious.

What is not 'diverse' is the rejection of the concept of a g-o-d who actively alters the course of natural events via episodic interventions – which of course is also compatible with much contemporary 'progressive' religious/Christian thought! But the question of the 'existence' of g-o-d is far from settled.

Nature[18] and naturalism are for us today 'the main game' for any progressive spirituality despite the continuing influence of neo-orthodoxy[19] within much denominational/church theology. If we think back over the past two centuries and recount the ways scientific knowledge has impacted our lives, what would top the list? I would suggest the recognition that nature is constitutive of who and what we are as human beings. "Whether or not we believe that there is something

---

[16] As a result, an issue for some is: can religious naturalism exist within more traditional faith communities?

[17] Names of past and present religious naturalists include Americans Henry Nelson Wieman, Bernard Loomer, and Bernard Meland. Other former religious naturalists include Samuel Alexander, Mordecai Kaplan, Ralph Burhoe, Thomas Berry, and Gordon Kaufman. Current ones include Karl Peters, Jerome Stone, Loyal Rue, Donald Crosby, Ursula Goodenough, Michael Cavanaugh, Michael S. Hogue, Sallie McFague, David Bumbaugh, Charlene Spretnak, Joanna Macy, Connie Barlow, and the later Lloyd Geering. Several are Unitarian in religious formation.

[18] Quote: "I take the term 'nature' to refer to the whole complex, interrelated and interacting unitary universe of matter-energy in space-time [which has emerged and evolved over a period of about 13.7 billion years into a complex of perhaps 100 billion galaxies, at least one of which contains perhaps 100 billion stars - some of which are surrounded by planets...], a universe of which humans are an integral part..." *(Gillette)*

[19] Emil Brunner wrote: "Because man has been made in the image of God, therefore he may and should make the earth subject to himself, and should have dominion over all other creatures... Man is only capable of realising his divine destiny when he rises above Nature". (Quoted in Geering. *The Greening of Christianity*, 43)

more", writes Lutheran systematic theologian Philip Hefner, "nature is so significant that all our beliefs must be reformulated so as to take nature into account." *(Hefner 2008:x)*

Given a chance, the cosmic evolution story – or 'New Story' – is too compelling, too beautiful, too edifying, and too liberating to fail in captivating the imagination of a vast majority of humankind. The human story and the universe story are the same story. We are not encapsulated, separated, isolated beings. Whatever we are, the universe is.

> "For just as the Milky Way is the universe in the form of a galaxy, and an orchid is the universe in the form of a flower, we are the universe in the form of a human. And every time we are drawn to look up into the night sky and reflect on the awesome beauty of the universe, we are actually the universe reflecting on itself." *(Thomas Berry)*

The capacity of the natural world to inspire a religious response from humans has long been recognised. Thus there is no good reason to believe that taking nature to heart leaves a person with any fewer spiritual benefits than taking to heart the teachings of *super*naturalist traditions.[20] "If we can go to special places, built by humans, which are designated as sacred," writes Jerome Stone,

> "surely we can go to special places, shaped naturally, which are recognized as sacred... There is a strong monotheistic tradition of cutting down the sacred groves. What we need is to realise that to have a sense of sacred place is not tree worship... but is rather the acknowledgement of the awesome, and the overriding and the overwhelming."[21]

---

[20] "...the dichotomy of natural/supernatural has now become obsolete. So far as I can ascertain we owe the use of the term supernatural to Aquinas as he tried to reconcile Christian thought with the rediscovered thought of Aristotle. In any case we now find ourselves in a world where nature reigns supreme. There is no supernatural sphere". (Lloyd Geering, Personal correspondence, 25/8/2016); Also Karl Peters, "Evolutionary Naturalism".

[21] Stone. "On Listening to Indigenous Peoples and Neo-pagans", 431. Lynn White: "To a Christian a tree can be no more than a physical fact. The whole concept of the sacred grove is alien to Christianity and to the ethos of the West. For nearly 2 millennia Christian missionaries have been chopping down sacred groves, which are idolatrous because they assume spirit in nature." (White. "The Historical Roots of our Ecological Crisis") See also Cusack *The Sacred Tree.*

Now... scholarly analysis and abstractions may burrow into and *challenge* our thinking, even *inspire* us. But as I have indicated elsewhere, facts and statistics are not enough. The shaping of progressive religious thought needs both the voice of the **scholarly critic** – to keep any community "athletically trim and free from a sloppy sentimentality"[22] – as well as the concern of the **creative artist** – to strike a chord and resonate within. Ideally the two should function 'in stereo' – simultaneous but quite different. *(Pierre Babin)* So, to substantially change how we feel we may need to participate in storytelling as well as some sort of *spiritual practice or ritual.*[23] The weaving of story (what we tell) and ritual (what we enact) are ways we make sense of our world.[24] Or, to put it another way: one gives us an oversight, the other gives us sight merged with smell and touch and terror... ways we make sense of the world.

> Dated somewhat now but back in the late 1960s when an ecological concern was first being given a public face, a ritual response to issues raised was being explored. Given the mundane name of 'tea-drinking', the ritual became part of several study and meditation groups on ecology/composting. The sessions began with the members drinking (billy) tea quietly and ceremonially while sitting on cushions.
>
> "Then the group moved on to an actual discussion in which practical techniques [concerning composting] and questions were aired. Finally, at the end of the meeting each person reverently sprinkled used tea leaves on the compost pile and took away a cup of half-finished compost and two worms. These items were seed for the compost pile that class members would later begin at home." *(Karl Peters)*

---

[22] Craddock. *Overhearing*..., 135.
[23] Donald Crosby expressed concern that there are currently "no rituals or ceremonies, no revered founders or scriptures, no stories, myths, and symbols" within religious naturalism. (Crosby, *quoted in Hogue* 2010:120-21)
[24] "... logical arguments will not persuade anyone who looks at nature and sees objects and mere resources. When perception is sufficiently changed, respectful types of conduct seem natural." (Stone. "Broadening Care..." quoting John Rodman.)

Commenting on this **past** ritual, Karl Peters wrote:

> "In such a ceremony the rational understanding of natural, ecological renewal is combined with ritual actions that may help establish new behaviour patterns in human beings."[25]

Ritual is more than a mind thing! It is an engagement.

- An example of how wonder and awe is being nurtured in meditation groups and eco-spiritual retreats **today**, is the Cosmic Walk, designed by Miriam MacGillis. A long rope is placed in a spiral, with 30 index cards representing the stages of evolution. Standing at the place of the first "Flaring Forth", the "pilgrims" are to reflect that they too are 14 billion years old. Likewise, they are invited to "enter" each great transition period in evolutionary history. At the end of the story when persons come out of the spiral, they call out their names: "The Universe has become Mary!" "The Universe has become James!"

Surely a liturgical link can be forged between naturalism and such feelings of wonder and awe in church worship/Sunday morning gatherings.[26] Indeed the annual Christian festivals of Christmas (sun) and Easter (moon), as well as the 'cross quarter days' between winter and summer solstice and spring and autumn equinox – all originated as festivals celebrating the changing seasons of nature, but were taken over by Christianity.[27]

Traditional theistic religion has long employed liturgical practices to instil *super*natural connotations by deploying music, theatre, incense, architecture and other ritual elements. Being no longer plausible, these

---

[25] Peters. "Humanity in Nature", 483-84.
[26] I acknowledge the natural environment can be both a spiritual resource and a spiritual competitor within the religio-spiritual marketplace with other, more traditional religious resources. See Ferguson & Tamburello. "The Natural Environment as a Spiritual Resource".
[27] "True [northern hemisphere] spring—warm reliable spring doesn't come [on March 21 or 22] until later. This is the cross quarter day - May 1 - which Europe celebrated with maypoles, gathering flowers, and fertility rites. May became the month of Mary after the Christian church took over and May crownings and processions were devoted to Mary instead of the old 'earth goddess'." *(LaChapelle)*

practices and ritual shaping should be absorbed and appreciated, but the *super*theology shaping such practices put aside.

Following biblical scholar and Westar Institute founder Robert Funk's suggestion,[28] I propose that a more radical *crafting* – something we 'bring' or 'create' – of ritual/liturgical rites is now required. Design a new Sunday Morning Experience from the ground up - with new music, new rituals, new scriptures, new ceremonies, new rites of passage all freed from restrictive creeds and dogmas and *super*naturalistic theology. Where congregants are invited to celebrate the wonder of the universe and the mystery of life, and to revere "the natural processes that have brought life into being and continue to sustain it." *(Lloyd Geering)* The goal of such a crafting is to arrive at a rich tapestry of language, metaphors, poetry, and design that (i) celebrates life in the present, (ii) can enrich such expressions of naturalistic beliefs,[29] and (iii) reflects we are people *of* the earth rather than people *on* the earth!

- The musicians and lyricists among us must continue to collaborate on new, more explicitly naturalistic songs and hymns. Limited attempts have been commenced, by such as Shirley Erena Murray, William L. Wallace, Jeff Guest, Bill Bennent, and Colin Gibson. These attempts need to be built on. For instance, a well-known traditional hymn suggests we are 'pilgrims through this barren land', but such words are demeaning of earth. Earth would surely respond: "If you read the landscape you will discover I am not 'barren' land [terra nullius] but an exciting ecosystem to be embraced and celebrated." *(Norman Habel)*

Keeping on the 'landscape' theme… Indigenous dreaming, for instance, is a tradition of story and ceremony, not a tradition of appeasement or offerings. The landscape itself is imbued with the

---

[28] Funk. "Editorial".
[29] "Underneath the surface of the various layers of Christianity lurk the remnants of religion that focused on nature. For example… we still name the days of the week after the ancient Germanic gods—Sunday for the sun-god, Monday for the moon-god, Wednesday for Woden, and Saturday for Saturn. These relics remain in spite of the efforts of priests to eliminate everything that smacked of superstitious paganism." *(Lloyd Geering)*

sacred.[30] A land-dreaming people.[31] Indigenous people have their own way of describing the fluidity of the seasons.

> "To this day, the Jawoyn people from the Northern Territory recognise six seasons. Other tribes measured time according to the rhythms of nature in their own areas and came up with different delineation. The unusual patterns of animals and birds or the flowering of plants were observed closely and became indicators of a change in the weather or a specific extreme such as a flood or drought."[32]

David Tacey claims the main language in Australia is earth language.

> "The sacred songs and chants [of Aboriginal peoples] are sung to gigantic and ancient rock formations and to vast expanses of red earth. The sacred dances are earth dances, where the celebrants gather to 'sing up' and sustain the spirits of the earth. Significantly, Aboriginal dance and celebration is concentrated upon the movements of the feet."[33]

Sure, there are those who dismiss all this as just being faddish, insisting that any genuinely Australian theology "must consist of more than just scattering kangaroos and gum trees across the page." Likewise, Australian sociologists "also know very well that over ninety per cent of Australians live in big cities near the coast, and rarely visit the desert, rainforest or countryside." *(Elizabeth Smith)* Yet I, along with others, claim being landscape-aware is being real to ordinary experience – the only grounds of a living tradition. Denis Edwards said on the Australian TV program *Compass* some years back:

---

[30] For Aboriginal people in Australia, religious identity is more a question of geography than theology.
[31] David Malouf. A Spirit of Play. Quoted in Leaves.
[32] Pilcher. "Marking Liturgical Time in Australia", 48.
[33] Tacey. Re-Enchantment, 96. See also LaChapelle. "Ritual is Essential"... "Most native societies around the world had three common characteristics: they had an intimate, conscious relationship with their place; they were stable 'sustainable' cultures, often lasting for thousands of years; and they had a rich ceremonial and ritual life."

"When the landscape is recognised as symbolic mediation of the healing and liberating of the Spirit then it becomes a place for encounter. Without recognition there is no human encounter and the landscape remains alien."
(Quoted in Ranson 1992)

- A challenge to artists and potters is to create liturgical artworks and artefacts that examine the beauty and spiritual meaning that can come from an appreciation of the natural world. In the past, I have been known to invite a potter to 'throw a pot' during a liturgy celebrating Spring. Or introduce liturgical dance and invite congregants to dance in the aisle! But, as one early American 'liberal' said: "Protestantism has been chary of the arts and suspicious of the artist." *(Von Ogden Vogt)*

- Stories and storytelling[34] are also important. Stories are an invitation rather than an argument. Storytelling helped us survive the rigours of natural selection, as it trained us to imagine the consequences of different possible scenarios for our actions. The prophetic voice of storyteller Thomas Berry:

> "...as we look up at the starry sky at night, and as, in the morning, we see the landscape revealed as the sun dawns over the earth – these experiences reveal a physical world but also a more profound world that cannot be bought with money, cannot be manufactured with technology, cannot be listed on the stock market, cannot be made in the chemical laboratory, cannot be reproduced with all our genetic engineering, cannot be sent by e-mail. These experiences require only that we follow the deepest feelings of the human soul."
> *(Thomas Berry/Swimme & Tucker 2011)*

---

[34] "Such people in the ancient Irish tradition... are called seanachies, which means story-catchers or story-sharers, and their job is *really important*, because stories are compass points and lodestars, and if we don't catch and share stories that matter, we will have nothing but lies and blood, and can't we do better than that?" *(Brian Doyle)*

And poets... of the calibre of Robert Weston and his beautiful "Out of the Stars..." and any of the poems of Pulitzer Prize-winning poet Mary Oliver, especially her "The Summer Day":

> "This grasshopper, I mean –
> the one who has flung herself out of the grass,
> the one who is eating sugar out of my hand..."[35]

These authors and others need to be re/introduced into our rituals and liturgies. Sticking with only readings and reflections from the Bible is too narrow a canon. Or to put it in the positive: religious naturalists affirm the importance of multiple sources of wisdom – old and new – for religious moral life.

- Celebrating the awe and wonder of the universe "and acknowledging our failures and misuse of other people and of the planet", some daring liturgists have produced special complete sacred rituals/liturgies. Three specifically come to mind... One is 'The Cosmic Mass'[36] (Matthew Fox, USA) – one liturgy per month – which begins with a "prolonged period during which participants experience and express awe through images, music, and movement".[37] A second is 'Sacred Energy: Mass of the Universe' (William L. Wallace, NZ) featuring prose, confession/lament, original choral and song,[38] "with accompanying power point presentation aiming to heighten the participants' sense of wonder and foster participation in the Mystery." The third is 'A Celtic Mass for Peace, Songs for the Earth' (Samuel Guarnaccia, USA), based on the writings of Celtic spirituality author, theologian, and poet, J. Philip Newell.[39]

---

[35] Mary Oliver... a mystic of the natural world, not a theologian of the church. Her theological orientation is not that of orthodox Christianity.

[36] The Mass follows the Four Paths of Creation Spirituality: *The Via Positiva* or celebration of existence (Thomas Aquinas says this is the first dimension to Worship: To say Thank You for Creation); the *Via Negativa* or sorrow for sins; the *Via Creativa*, the blessing of wine and bread as the food of the Cosmic Christ; and the Sending Off which is the *Via Transformativa*.

[37] Fox claims we should fall in love at least three times each day with something like a galaxy, a tree, our cat, or a song. Sanguin. *Darwin, Divinity...*, 249.

[38] https://progressivechristianity.org/

[39] https://store.cdbaby.com/cd/samuelguarnaccia

Perhaps the stand-out example of such celebrations within the 'progressive' Christian tradition is the Cathedral of St John the Divine in New York City. The Cathedral hosts resident artists and artistic companies, while its celebrations of winter and summer solstices have become so popular that tens of thousands pilgrimage each year to participate in services led by African drummers, nationally known jazz musicians, resident theatre and dance groups, and an ever expanding spectrum of artists. *(Hal Taussig)*

Two general liturgical collections may also prove helpful:
(i) Diann Neu probes the inter-relatedness of ecology and feminism using the framework of the four seasons,[40] and
(ii) Australian Norman Habel's *Rainbow of Mysteries* explores "where and how [we] might resonate with the spiritual in creation, meet the sacred in nature, and live as Earth's spiritual partner".[41]

In my most recent book, *When Progressives Gather Together: Liturgy, Lectionary, Landscape... And Other Explorations*,[42] I offer commentary and liturgical examples grounded in both a religious naturalism and a celebration of life. One such example comes out of my reshaping of the 'Words of Committal' from the Funeral Liturgy – often the most common 'public' event with echoes of 'religion'...

The spirit of (NNN) shall not know the blight of mortality:
for it shall live on in the lives made real
   by its presence, and its gracious influence.

Those atoms and molecules which constituted
his/her physical frame...
Every one of them originated in the burst of heat and light
   which created our galaxy millions of light years ago.

---

[40] Neu. *Returned Blessings.*
[41] Habel. *Rainbow of Mysteries*, 17.
[42] 2016. Morning Star Publishing.

They persisted in bodies both animate and inanimate
that came into being on planet Earth,
   and they reached their fulfilment in the generous life-form
   and personality of this strong,
      courageous, self conscious human being, we called (N).

So reverently, lovingly, trustingly,
we commit his/her body to the elements/to the ground,
   which is welcoming to us at the time of our death.
Ashes to ashes/earth to earth, star dust to star dust.

In the cycle of life and death
the earth is replenished
   and life is eternally renewed.

Vietnamese Zen Buddhist Thich Nhat Hanh reminds us similarly:

"Earth brings us to life and nourishes us.
Earth takes us back again.
Birth and death are present in every moment."

With the increased use of cremation over burial[43] many families and relatives are now considering the additional ritual of *interment of ashes* (with a biodegradable urn) of a deceased loved one, at a latter date, rather than just *scattering the ashes* sometime, somewhere. Another common action is the planting of a tree or some other sort of planting in a public space – park, arboretum, community garden, bush setting, beach – all possibilities for associating the deceased with nature or appreciation of nature.

oo0oo

The chief mark of 'religion', according to idealist philosopher William Ernest Hocking (1873-1966), is not unity but fertility.[44] Religion is the 'mother' of all the great cultural interests of human life. But it lives

---

[43] Traditionally the Christian church has advocated burial since its inception. It reserved burning for witches and other so-called heretics.

[44] Hocking. *The Meaning of God...*, 13-15.

only while we are making it up, while our imaginations and creative juices are firing and we are generating – crafting *(religiopoiesis)* – new angles, new narratives, new metaphors within the particular context of the moment because these things are liberating.

Yet, traditional *theistic* religion conditions its adherents to see tradition as fixed, magic where there is none, and miracle when the story is the common, everyday thing. Why? The answer may lie in the all-too-common error of taking for granted those things that are both simple and natural.

So, where to start personally?[45] Start by taking a three-year-old child (maybe your grand-daughter or grandson) for a walk along some wet-lands track and witness her innate delight in all she beholds. Do not plan to be in a hurry. The delight experienced by her will be the delight with the particular: every leaf, every coloured stone, every duck, every small grasshopper, snail, or lizard to cross your path... All occasions for closer 'looking' and excitement. Such is the aesthetic, the enchantment of a three year old for the natural world.[46] Traditional theistic religion, obsessed with sin, causes us to pay attention to what is wrong. The challenge is to offer a new kind of centrality: notice what is wonderful and refreshing! "We rarely take the time to appreciate our eyes..." suggests Thich Nhat Hanh again, "We only need to open our eyes, and we see every kind of form and color – the blue sky, the beautiful hills, the trees, the clouds, the rivers, the children, the butterflies." (*Thick That Hanh* 2001:21-22)

Start with your own life. With the 37.2 trillion cells of your body that are converting energy to make protein right now so that you can read these words. Or... with the awareness that the body you are carrying around now – an "original, impermanent compound

---

[45] When an similar earlier version of this paper was part of an oral presentation, those attending were invited to look at the moon on their exiting the hall... That night (14 November 2016) it was the closest full moon to earth so far in the 21st century. It would not be that close again until 23 November 2034.

[46] Cell biologist Ursula Goodenough writes: "That we possess as part of our genetic heritage an aesthetic for the natural is readily affirmed by taking a young child for a walk in the woods or by the sea and witnessing her innate delight in all she beholds. The delight has little to do with sunsets or vistas, with order or pattern or purpose. The delight is with the particular: the ladybug crawling on the rock, the fuzzy moss, the tickly dunegrass, the mucky mud by the river. Children connect with the immediate and become a part of it. The mud isn't messy, or rather, its messiness is what makes it wonderful. Children are inherently attuned to Nature."

of disappearingly smaller parts" *(Paul Fleischman)* – won't be the body you'll be carrying around three, five, seven years from now. It will have completely rebuilt itself from the inside out. "If you want to know where the environment is, just feel yourself," suggests religious philosopher Jerome Stone...

> "That is where the environment is. The skin is not a wall around us. The skin, the lungs, the digestive tract are permeable membranes designed to let the environment in. So we ignore the environment at our peril."[47]

Start by taking some time to view the DVD 'Journey of the Universe', narrated by Brian Swimme, and honouring the work of Thomas Berry, celebrating the notion that

> "environmental concerns are best addressed when we recognize our origins and evolutionary history, when we understand that we are participants in and not observers of nature – enabling our ability to cherish and protect what continues to nourish us."[48]

Allow yourself to be shaped by this creativity. This wonder. Webs of culture, life, and cosmos, "resulting in unending successions of ever-evolving levels of living forms." *(Karl Peters)* Each day "lifts its head from the dew-strung grasses and offers new hope, new possibilities, extra chances" *(Gretta Vosper)* because every moment is pregnant with possibility. The miracle of each moment awaits our sensual wonder. Hosannah! Not in the highest, but right here. Right now. This.[49] Horizontal transcendence. Nature embedded in humanity. Humanity embedded in nature. *Of, in,* and *as* nature.

The sacred is *not* a separate '*super*natural' sphere of life, driven by blinding-light revelations. "Out of almost unlimited potential," writes Paul Fleischman,

---

[47] Stone. "Inaugural Liberal Arts Lecture".
[48] Goodenough. "Journey of the Universe".
[49] Goodenough. *The Sacred Depths...*, 169.

"life is that which was selected over long times and many circumstances. Positing an incomprehensible, invisible, 'Other' does nothing to explain the incomprehensible 'other' that is palpably present, and that we actually *encounter every second within and around us*".[50]

Neither is the sacred to be found separate from the pursuits of truth, justice, beauty and selfhood. It is more like the caffeine in coffee than like a strawberry on top of the pavlova. So what does religious *experience* look and feel like from the standpoint of religious naturalism? A formal explanation from Michael Hogue is helpful:

"Religious experiences for the religious naturalist provoke questions about the meanings and values that ultimately orient life – they are interrogative rather the declarative. They are events, encounters, insights, relationships, undergoings, and overcomings that throw life into suspense, stripping away the pretence of the givenness of things, compelling one, even if just for a moment, to face the contingency of what is taken to be necessary, the vulnerability of what is taken to be invulnerable, and the perishability of what is assumed to be permanent. Experiences such as these throw life into a new frame; they rend the veil of the ordinary. They interrupt and can sometimes transform one's life."[51]

Let me be clear: religious naturalism will not save the traditional institutional *church*. That theology continues to be embalmed in neo-orthodoxy, and in denominational terms, is almost certainly terminal. My Canadian colleague, Gretta Vosper, is far more direct (and honest):

"I have no illusions about where the church is headed; like all Christian denominations, it will either wear itself out or veer back, dramatically, to the right and become, as religion always does, a sedative in the coming trauma of human existence. That sounds bleak. It is." *(Vosper 2017)*

---

[50] Fleischman. *Wonder*, 188.
[51] Hogue. "Religion Without God", 15-16.

Sections of 'orthodoxy' see no need to work at reforming the church to reverse this decline because it is the world that is the problem, not the church and its practices and theology. It is however, the hope of a growing number of people (often outside the church institution) that religious naturalism, the 'forgotten alternative', will prevail as the most universal, open, and suggestive *religious orientation* on the planet, whatever one's traditional religion. But it also needs to be said: RN is not nearly as 'marketable' as traditional church neo-orthodoxy, "since it doesn't promise perks like eternal life, etc." *(Ursula Goodenough)*

Developments with a promise for a very different future are being explored by a new wave of religious naturalists as they engage the religious and moral urgencies of the present. It is not just an 'explosion of imagination' that is exciting new participants, it is also the belonging to a group experimenting with a new social vision that is attractive. Of that new wave and new vision, Loyal Rue suggests that today's religious naturalists...

> "will be known for their reverence and awe before Nature, their love for Nature and natural forms, their sympathy for all living things, their guilt for enlarging the ecological footprints, their pride in reducing them, their sense of gratitude directed towards the matrix of life, their contempt for those who abstract themselves from natural values, and their solidarity with those who link their self-esteem to sustainable living." *(Loyal Rue)*

Whether all this is called 'religion' or 'spirituality' or so-called 'secular mysticism' I am not really too fussed. Molecular/cell biologist Ursula Goodenough has this take on this oft-times debate: it is the integration of the theology and the spirituality that forms the matrix of a viable religious orientation.

> "[T]he theology alone is dry as dust; the spirituality alone is self-absorbed, even autistic."[52]

---

[52] Goodenough. "Exploring Resources of Naturalism". Also "Religiopoiesis" where she states: "Indeed, one of the important insights from contemporary neurobiology is that these distinctions are at least partially false: without an emotional or intuitive component, theological/philosophical issues may have no meaning to the thinker in the sense that s/he will not be able to assign value or importance to alternative outcomes."

More of a concern for me is that both religious thought and 'natural' liturgy/ritual respond to the challenges framed by ecological scientists and progressive religion scholars. And the key role of the place-time 'fit'. In a time of ecological vulnerability and dislocation of the social fabric, contemporary religious naturalism's conceptions of and attitudes toward nature and religiosity have much to commend it. Especially its willingness to entertain radically new approaches, "and explore trackless places and experiences" *(Michael Hogue)* as it engages with some of the most pressing religious and moral issues at the core of the ecological crisis. Because...

> "the miracle is not to walk on water.
> The miracle is to walk on the green Earth in the present moment,
> to appreciate the peace and beauty
> that is available now." (*Thich Nhat Hanh*, 1996:367)

Bibliography

Anderson, H. & E. Foley. **Mighty Stories, Dangerous Rituals. Weaving Together the Human and the Divine**. San Francisco. Jossey-Bass Publishers, 1998

Axel, L. E. *"Reshaping the Task of Theology"* in William Dean. (ed). The Size of God. The Theology of Bernard Loomer in Context, published in **American Journal of Theology & Philosophy 8**, 1 & 2, January & May 1987

Axel, R. C. *"Meland and Loomer: Forging an Alternative to Patriarchal Secularism"* in W. C. Peden & L. E. Axel. (ed). **New Essays in Religious Naturalism**. Highlands Institute Series 2. Georgia. Mercer University Press, 1993

Babin, P. **The New Era in Religious Communication**. (Translated by David Smith). Minneapolis. Fortress Press, 1991

Barrett, J. E. *"Pragmatism, Process, and Courage"* in W. C. Peden & L. E. Axel. (ed). **New Essays in Religious Naturalism**. Highlands Institute Series 2. Georgia. Mercer University Press, 1993

Berry, T. "Evening Thoughts" in M. E Tucker & J. Grim. (ed). **Thomas Berry: Selected Writings on the Earth Community**. New York. Orbis Books, 2014

– – – – –, *"The Dream of the Earth"* quoted in L. G. Geering. **The Greening of Christianity**. Wellington. St Andrew's Trust, 2005

Bumbaugh, D. *"Toward a Humanist Vocabulary of Reverence"*. Boulder International Humanist Institute, Fourth Annual Symposium, Boulder, Colorado. 22 February 2003. (Accessed 20 December 2015). <http://www.uua.org/sites/live-new.uua.org/files/documents/bumbaughdavid/humanist_reverence.pdf>

Butler Bass, D. **Grounded: Finding God in the World. A Spiritual Revolution**. New York. HarperOne, 2015

Craddock, F. **Overhearing the Gospel**. Nashville. Abingdon Press, 1978

Crosby, D. **More Than Discourse: Symbolic Expressions of Naturalistic Faith**. New York. SUNY Press, 2015

Cusack, C. M. **The Sacred Tree: Ancient and Medieval Manifestations**. Newcastle-upon-Tyne. Cambridge Scholars Press, 2011

Drees, W. B. *"Thick Naturalism: Comments on Zygon 2000"*, **Zygon 35**, 4, (December 2000), 856

Ferguson, T. W. & J. A. Tamburello. *"The Natural Environment as a Spiritual Resource: A Theory of Regional Variation in Religious Adherence"* in **Sociology of Religion 76**, 3, (2015), 295-314

Fleischman, P. R. **Wonder: When and Why the World Appears Radiant**. Amherst. Small Batch Books, 2013

Funk, R. *"Editorial"* in **The Fourth R 18**, 1, (2005), 2, 20

Geering, L. G. **Reimagining God. The Faith Journey of a Modern Heretic.**

Salem. Polebridge Press, 2014

– – – – –, **From the Big Bang to God. An Awe-Inspiring Journey of Evolution**. Salem. Polebridge Press, 2013

– – – – –, **Coming Back to Earth. From gods, to God, to Gaia**. Salem. Polebridge Press, 2009

– – – – –, **The Greening of Christianity**. Wellington. St Andrew's Trust, 2005

Gillette, P. R. *"Theology Of, By, & For Religious Naturalism"* in **The Journal of Liberal Religion 6**, 1, 2006

Goodenough, U. *"Evolution is Not About Survival of the Fittest But About Fitting In."* A Sermon, preached at The First Unitarian Church of Alton. (No date). <www.firstuualton.org>

– – – – –, *"'Journey of the Universe': The Challenge of Telling Everybody's Story"*, **13.7 Cosmos & Culture: Commentary on Science and Society** web site, 31 March 2011 (Accessed April 2017)

– – – – –, *"Vertical and Horizontal Transcendence"* in **Zygon 36**, 1, (March 2001),

– – – – –, *"Exploring Resources of Naturalism: Religiopoiesis"* in **Zygon 35**, 3, (September 2000), 352 - 355

– – – – –, **The Sacred Depths of Nature**. New York: Oxford University Press, 1998

Habel, N. C. **Rainbow of Mysteries: Meeting the Sacred in Nature**. Kelowna. CopperHouse/Wood Lake Publishing, 2012

– – – – –, **An Inconvenient Text: Is a Green Reading of the Bible Possible?** Hindmarsh. ATF Press, 2009

Hanh, Thich Nhat. **Essential Writings**. (Ed). Robert Ellsberg. Maryknoll. Orbis Books, 2001

– – – – –, *"Present Moment Wonderful Moment"* in E. Roberts & E. Amidon. **Life Prayers from Around the World. 365 Prayers, Blessings, and Affirmations to Celebrate the Human Journey**. New York. HarperCollins, 1996

– – – – –, *"Earth Brings us Life..."* in E. Roberts & E. Amidon. **Earth Prayers from Around the World. 365 Prayers, Poems, and Invocations for Honoring the Earth**. New York. HarperCollins, 1991

Hefner, P. "Forward" in J. A. Stone. **Religious Naturalism Today. The Rebirth of a Forgotten Alternative**. New York. SUNY Press, 2008

Hocking, W. E. **The Meaning of God in Human Experience. A Philosophic Study of Religion**. New Haven. Yale University Press, 1912/1963

Hogue, M. S. *"Religion Without God: The Way of Religious Naturalism"* in **The Fourth R 27**, 3, (May-June 2014), 3-6, 15-16

– – – – –, **The Promise of Religious Naturalism**. Lanham. Rowman & Littlefield Publishers, 2010

Hunt, R. A. E. **When Progressives Gather Together: Liturgy, Lectionary, Landscape… And Other Explorations**. Northcote. Morning Star Publishing, 2016

– – – – -, & J. W. H. Smith. (ed). **Why Weren't We Told: A Handbook on Progressive Christianity**. Oregon. Polebridge Press, 2012

Keen, S. **In the Absence of God. Dwelling in the Presence of the Sacred**. Edinburgh. Harmony Publishing, 2010

LaChapelle, D. *"Ritual is Essential. Seeing Ritual and Ceremony as Sophisticated Social and Spiritual Technology"* in **In Context**, 5, (Spring 1984), 39

Loomer, B. M. *"The Size of God"* in William Dean. (ed). The Size of God. The Theology of Bernard Loomer in Context, published in **American Journal of Theology & Philosophy 8**, 1 & 2, January & May 1987. (Also published separately)

McEmrys, A. *"Living Liturgy: A Unitarian-Universalist Liturgical Theology in Theory and Practice"* in **The Journal of Liberal Religion 6**, 1, 2006

MacGillis, M. *"The Cosmic Walk"*. A resource posted on <http://www.greenfaith.org/> (Accessed February 2017)

Neu, D. L. **Return Blessings: Ecofeminist Liturgies Renewing the Earth**. Cleveland: Pilgrim Press, 2002

"Painting the Stars: Science, Religion and an Evolving Faith." DVD/Video. Produced by **Living the Questions**, 2013

Peters, K. E. "Toward an Evolutionary Christian Theology" in **Zygon 42**, 1, (March 2007), 49-63

– – – – -, **Dancing with the Sacred: Evolution, Ecology, and God**. Harrisburg. Trinity Press International, 2002

– – – – -, *"Storytellers and Scenario Spinners: Some Reflections on Religion and Science in light of a Pragmatic, Evolutionary Theory of Knowledge"* in **Zygon 32**, 4, (December 1997), 465-489

– – – – -, *"Interrelating Nature, Humanity, and the Work of God: Some Issues for Future Reflection"* in **Zygon 27**, 4, (December 1992), 403-419

– – – – -, *"Humanity in Nature: Conserving Yet Creating"* in **Zygon 24**, 4, (December 1989), 469-485

– – – – -, *"Evolutionary Naturalism: Survival as a Value"* in **Zygon 15**, 2, (June 1980), 213-222

Pilcher, C. *"Marking Liturgical Time in Australia: Pastoral Considerations"* in S. Burns & A. Monro. (ed). **Christian Worship in Australia. Inculturating the Liturgical Tradition**. Strathfield. St Paul's Publications, 2009

Preston, N. *"Eco-Theology: The Main Game for Religious Progressives"* in R. A. E. Hunt & G. C. Jenks. (ed). **Wisdom and Imagination: Religious Progressives and the Search for Meaning**. Northcote. Morning Star Publishing, 2014

– – – – -, *"Exploring Eco-Theology"* in R. A. E. Hunt & J. W. H. Smith. (ed). **Why Weren't We Told? A Handbook on 'progressive' Christianity.** Salem. Polebridge Press, 2013

Primack, J. R. & N. E. Abrams. **The View from the Centre of the Universe. Discovering our Extraordinary Place in the Cosmos.** New York. Riverhead Books, 2006

Ranson, D. *"Fire in Water. The Liturgical Cycle in the Experience of South East Australian Seasonal Patterns"* in **Compass Theology Review** 26, 1992. (Photocopy in private circulation).

"Religious Naturalism. A Religious Worldview Grounded in the Sciences, the Humanities, and the Arts". https://religiousnaturalism.org/what-is-religious-naturalism/ (Accessed August 2016)

Rue, L. **Religion Is Not About God.** New Brunswick. Rutgers University Press, 2006

Smith, E. J. *"Crafting and Singing Hymns in Australia"* in S. Burns & A. Monro. (ed). **Christian Worship in Australia. Inculturating the Liturgical Tradition.** Strathfield. St Paul's Publications, 2009

Spearritt, G. *"Religion: It's Natural!"*. (No date). Sea of Faith in Australia. <www.sof-in-australia.org/religion.htm> (Accessed December 2001)

Stone, J. A. **Sacred Nature: The Environmental Potential of Religious Naturalism.** New York. Routledge, 2017

– – – – -, **Religious Naturalism Today. The Rebirth of a Forgotten Alternative.** New York. SUNY Press, 2008

– – – – -, *"Is God Emeritus? The Idea of God Among Religious Naturalists"* in **The Journal of Liberal Religion 5**, 1, 2005

– – – – -, *"Is Nature Enough? Yes"* in **Zygon 38**, 4, (December 2003) 783-800

– – – – -,*"What is Religious Naturalism?"* in **The Journal of Liberal Religion 2**, 1, 2000

– – – – -, *"Inaugural Liberal Arts Lecture"*, 1998, William Harper College, Chicago, quoted in M. S Hogue. **The Promise of Religious Naturalism.** Lanham. Rowman & Littlefield Publishers, 2010

– – – – -, *"On Listening to Indigenous Peoples and Neo-pagans: Obstacles to Appropriating the Old Ways"* in C. D. Hardwick & D. A. Crosby. (ed). **Pragmatism, Neo-Pragmatism, and Religion: Conversations with Richard Rorty.** New York. Peter Lang, 1997

– – – – -, *"Broadening Care, Discerning Worth: The Environmental Contributions of Minimalist Religious Naturalism"* in **Process Studies 22**, 4, (Winter 1993), 194-203

– – – – -, **The Minimalist Vision of Transcendence. A Naturalist Philosophy of Religion.** Albany. State University of New York Press, 1992

Sanguin, B. **Darwin, Divinity, and the Dance of the Cosmos. An Ecological**

Christianity. Kelowna. Copper House/Wood Lake Publishing, 2007

Swimme, B. T. & M. E. Tucker. **Journey of the Universe**. New Haven. Yale University Press, 2011

Tacey, D. **ReEnchantment: The New Australian Spirituality**. Pymble. HarperCollins, 2000

Taussig, H. **A New Spiritual Home: Progresive Christianity at the Grass Roots**. Santa Rosa: Polebridge Press, 2006

– – – – -, *"Ritual Theory Applied to 21st Century Christian Worship Practices"*. A paper distributed to members of the Literacy & Liturgy Seminar, Westar Institute, 2006 (In private circulation)

Vogt, V. O. **Modern Worship**. Lowell Institute Lectures. New Haven. Yale University Press, 1927

– – – – -, **Art and Religion**. New Haven. Yale University Press, 1921. (Second printing 1929)

Vosper, G. "Question and Answer". Guest contributor to Bishop John Shelby Spong's newsletter, **A New Christianity for a New World**, (7 September 2017), On-line.

– – – – -, **We All Breathe. Poems and Prayers**. Toronto. File 14. PostPurgical Resources, 2012

White Jr, L. *"The Historical Roots of our Ecological Crisis"* in **Science 155**, 3767, (March 1967) <science.sciencemag.org>

Theme focus: Seasons

1. SEASONS AND SELF...

> "Winter is nature's way of saying, 'Up yours'."
> *(Robert Byrne)*

It is said no one says much good of winter.
Except as something hard that exaggerates the Spring reprieve.
    No one says much of it.
    It just is.

Take trees for instance.
If those trees are the imported kind, their coloured clown suits of leaves
    will have already turned winter brown or yellow,
    and as if to sacrifice their life,
        fallen to the ground to become spring fertiliser.

Take snow for instance.
We don't get snow on the coast. That's reserved for hills and further inland. On farming land.
    Indeed, it used to be said farmers called snow 'the poor man's fertiliser'.
    It was next year's water.
    It was next year's crop.

Take grass for instance.
My front lawn has a strong brown tinge to it
as it copes with cold frost-like mornings.
    But amid it all several pestilent patches of green weed-grass
    are making a bold protest.
        Remember us! they seem to say.

Dull. Cold. Bare.
No one says much good of winter…
       ooOoo

Seasons are as much a cultural phenomenon as food, music, religion and dance.
In reality, the delineation of the year into four seasons – Spring, Summer, Autumn, Winter –
> is as arbitrary as starting them on the first of a certain month.
> (*Phillips* 2014)

Due to its size, there is not one single seasonal calendar for the entire Australian continent.
According to the Bureau of Meteorology the temperature can range
> from below zero in the Snowy Mountains in southern Australia,
> to extreme heat in the Kimberley region in the north-west of the continent.

Over all, summer is the warmest season of the year, falling between spring and autumn.
Warm weather, days at the beach, and the start of an extended holiday period
> herald summer's 'southern' arrival.

According to 'astronomical summer' the season occurs on or around December 22 in the Southern Hemisphere,
> when the South Pole is tilted toward the sun,
> and when night and day are approximately the same length.

But there is another definition for summer.
A meteorological season is defined as the 12 months of the year
> being divided up into four season with three months each.

June, July and August are considered summer, north of the equator, while December, January and February are summer to the south.
> Which of course means the latter makes for a different/ interesting Christmas!

By contrast, the southern Hobart 'winter' brings with it overcoats, beanies, and umbrellas...
And on at least one occasion - snow on a summer Christmas Day!
>But up north, in Darwin, an average winter (or 'the dry') temperature is often more than 31 degrees celsius.

As southern states folk like to whine: how that qualifies as 'winter' is anyone's guess!

Then there are the between-times.
Autumn's gone but winter has not quite come
>calendars to the contrary...

People tend always to read, think, and understand
from their particular place on the planet.
>But it goes further.

The natural seasons not only have symbolic value they also affect us physiologically.
Seasonal changes in temperature, sunlight,
>precipitation, barometric pressure, and lunar cycles
>all have demonstrable effects on our moods and physical functioning.

ooOoo

Indigenous Australians have a different system of seasons according to whereabouts in Australia they are from.
Close to where I was born and raised is a low mountain range called the Grampians, or the *Gariwerd*, home of the *Djab Wurrung* and *Jardwidjarli* clans.

These clans do not have specific names or dates for the seasons such as autumn or winter, instead their six seasons were described
>by what was happening at the time.
>>'The wattles are now flowering so we know that the eels are on the move'.

Other clans came up with a different delineation according to the rhythms of nature in their own areas:
> The *Walabunnba* people from north of Alice Springs
> has three seasons. But some kilometres north
> > the *Jawoyn* people from the Katherine, has six.

The actual length or timing of the season depended on the environment and climate.

> "The unusual patterns of animals and birds or the flowering of plants were observed closely and became indicators of a change in the weather or a specific extreme such as a flood or drought."

ooOoo

Like Earth, we too have our seasons marked by change and often best reflected upon by the poets and liturgists in our midst.
Because human beings are 'storytellers and scenario spinners'.
> "Now I am not so very young,
> and time runs faster that it did.
> > am much more mortal than I was at ten...

"It takes a little while to know how much of life is death
and not to dread it so.
> To sense the equilibrium of the earth,
> To be at home in time, and take the limits
> > of both life and love..." *(Coots 1971:61, 62)*

As one grows older it is often referred to as entering the 'autumn years'.
The younger version of me always dreaded the idea of growing older.
> But now that I have not only knocked on autumn's door,
> but opened the door and taken a few steps inside,
> > I admit to being some-what pleased to have made it this far!

"No matter how old one is," writes *HuffingtonPost* blogger, Judith Rich,

> "we're always standing at the edge of the unknown. There is no certainty, not even about taking the next breath. But growing older affords one a certain perspective on life, not available from the earlier parts of the journey. Gratitude comes forward, front and center, as the prevailing consciousness. What could be better than that?" *(Rich 2011)*

New birth is a time for public celebration, and sometimes those celebrations are centred around Baptism or Thanksgiving/ Naming ceremonies.

In my own Baptism liturgy, I use the elements of water and fragrant oil (tradition) and earth (naturalism).

Water:
"For us in Australia, the driest continent on earth, water is a precious commodity...
   Water is everything.
   Water is life.

"(NNN) in the touch of this water, the ancient symbol of new life,
I baptise you into the love, service and joy of God:
   Father, Son, and Holy Spirit...
   Source of Life, Companion, Enlivener."
(Water is poured over the head of the child)

Fragrant Oil:
"Take this name and make it your own.
Live in freedom and fullness

"We anoint you with fragrant oil
as a sign of our blessing to you this day.
   May you grow in wisdom and understanding.

(touch head with oil)
May you work for justice in the world.
(touch hands)
May you walk in the ways of peace."
(touch feet)

Earth:
"Respecting the relationship between humankind and
the earth insight of Aboriginal people,
   (N), we place your feet in this soil.

You are a child of the Spirit and a child of the Earth.
You have inherited the responsibility of caring for this earth.
   Cherish it for all creation." *(Hunt 2016)*

An overseas colleague, in his "Blessings at a Naming Ceremony for a Baby" ceremonies, also takes seriously one's place in the universe by acknowledging the elements of our common being.

"(The speaker lifts a handful of earth before the child)
With earth, which is as solid as your given frame, my child,
   we bless you.
Take care of yourself as a body,
be good to yourself, for you are a good gift…"

The liturgy continues, acknowledging air and fire, finishing with water…
"(The speaker dips fingers into warm water and touches them to the crown of the child's head.)
With water, which is clear as your spirit, my child,
   we bless you.
Grow in conscience, be rooted in good stories,
grow spiritually, for spirit too is a good gift." *(Belletini 1996:187)*

He also tells of the 'flower' surprise he would receive around Mother's Day each year...

> "My sermon begins simply enough, with a flower on my desk. Each year for ten years, when I entered my former office at my church in Hayward, California on Mothers' Day, I found a gorgeous flower in a vase on my desk. It could have been a peony... or a rose. But it was always a single blossom. And propped against the vase was always a card, which read "Happy Mother's Day."
>
> "It was never signed. I never caught anyone leaving it, no matter how early I showed up in the morning. But it was always there.
>
> "I never knew who left it. I never found out why whoever left it, left it. But even though I am, obviously, technically not a mother, I always was delighted by it, and took it as a very sweet and honoring gesture." *(Belletini 2001)*

And then comes the end of life as we know it.
Death. Our death.
Few people think about death. Their own death, that is.
It is considered a taboo subject.
>When it is talked about, most of the time the conversation
>is shaped around death as an abstract principle - a dispassionate
>facet of Life.

But when death becomes personal through someone we have known, respected, and loved, it comes in a variety of guises
>and triggers varying emotions.,

As a progressive and a religious naturalist
my understanding of the universe is,
the natural world is all there is.
>Death is part of the life process.
>There is no heaven and no afterlife.
>This life is all there is.

Traditional and fundamentalist Christians will blame all this on Charles Darwin,
but there is no scientific evidence of anything *super*natural.
> Neither is there any credible evidence that humankind
>> is a unique creation by a deity,
>>> nor any basis for the existence of a 'soul'.

On the other hand, this doesn't mean our living will not be remembered.
As my own Funeral liturgy says:
> "The gifts and graces which s/he offered are never lost to us.
> The creativity which s/he brought to us
> in her/his life and relationships
>> lies now within our own lives
>> and travels into the future with us.
> Our lives have been changed because we lived with him/her."

And again in the Words of Committal from that liturgy:
> "The spirit of (NNN)
> shall not know the blight of mortality:
> for it shall live on in the lives made real
>> by its presence, and its gracious influence.

> "Those atoms and molecules which constitute his/her physical frame...
> Every one of them originated in the burst of heat and light
>> which created our galaxy millions of light years ago.

> "They persisted in bodies both animate and inanimate
> that came into being on planet Earth,
>> and they reached their fulfilment in the generous life-form
>> and personality of this strong,
>>> courageous, self conscious human being, we called (N).
> So reverently, lovingly, trustingly..." *(Hunt 2016)*

So it matters far more to come to terms with our end
than to be preoccupied with 'metaphysical speculation'
> about what might lie beyond this life.
>> "Death is present and palpable, a matter of evidence. Not only are there no good grounds for anticipating immortality, but also doing so distracts us from the life that we do have." *(Aronson 2008:151)*

We all die.
And all of us dies.

The words of playwright William Shakespeare may suffice for now even as most of us will need to return to this emotive subject often:
> 'Cowards die many times before their deaths
> The valiant never taste of death but once.
> Of all the wonders that I yet have heard
> It seems to me most strange that men should fear
> Seeing that death, a necessary end,
> Will come when it will come.'

Perhaps these 'seasons of the self' could in part be summed up in the words of New Zealander Shirley Erena Murray's contemporary song...
> "Our life has its seasons
> and God has the reasons
> why spring follows winter,
> and new leaves grow,
> for there's a connection
> with our resurrection
> that flowers will bud
> after frost and snow... *(Murray 1993)*

ooOoo

Karl Peters, retired professor of philosophy and religion, has a couple of other interesting, if detailed, comments about our 'seasons' and 'self'. He writes:

"We contain in us – in all of ourselves after many cosmic, biological, and cultural transformations – the radiation that was present at the origin of the universe."

He then proceeds to ask the question: 'How old are we?' His response:

> "[p]henomenally, a few decades; culturally, a few centuries or millennia; biologically, millions of years; cosmically, about 15 billion years."
> *(Peters 1992:412)*

To the additional question: 'How long will we continue?' Peters adds:

> "[p]henomenally, a few more decades or less; culturally, maybe a few more centuries; biologically, millions of years or, if we do not destroy ourselves first, perhaps until our sun dies five (5 billion years from now; cosmically, until the universe ends, which may be never... It all depends on how we think of our selves." *(Peters 1992:412)*

Peters answers are a kind of cosmic recipe for the functioning of all things.
And reminds us that the seasons of nature is in us
as much as we are nature.

> "We are webs of reality, woven out of the threads of culture, biology, and cosmos... As webs of reality each of us is a manifestation of a larger part of the universe as a whole..."
> *(Peters 1992:412)*

When I think of my own life – my own 'seasons' – I know
I want to exist as long as I can in a healthy way in my present state,
    fulfilling the possibilities of my own existence, and
        contributing positively to my culture, to my grandchildren,
            and to the environment.

And at centre stage is a sense of wonder and acts of celebration.
The world – a circus of forms – of gum leaves and desert rocks and butterflies, and human fingers with or without arthritis.

The celebration of life – the whole of life.
And dumbstruck by golden wattles in early spring!
>"The village clock keeps time as time should be,
>But I blaspheme Old Chronos with months I make
>and seasons entered in myself.

"My year:
>A year that is my life-
>A life that is my time-
>My time that ought to be eternity enough." *(Coots 1971:10)*

Notes

Aronson, R. **Living Without God. New Directions for Atheists, Agnostics, Secularists, and the Undecided.** Berkeley. Counterpoint, 2008.

Belletini, M. *"Blessings at a Naming Ceremony for a Baby"* in Roberts, E. & E. Amidon. (ed). **Life Prayers from Around the World. 365 Prayers, Blessings, and Affirmations to Celebrate the Human Journey.** New York. HarperCollins, 1996.

Belletini, M. *"Mother's Day"*, Sermon. First Unitarian Universalist Church of Columbus, Ohio. 13 May 2001. <firstcols.org> (Accessed August 2017).

Coots, M. **Seasons of the Self.** Nashville. Abingdon, 1971.

Hunt, R. A. E. **When Progressives Gather Together: Liturgy, Lectionary, Landscape… And Other Explorations.** Northcote. Morning Star Publishing, 2016.

Murray, S. E. *"Our Life has its Seasons"* No. 113 **Alleluia Aotearoa. Hymns and Songs for all Churches.** Raumati. New Zealand Hymnbook Trust, 1993.

Peters, K. E. 1992. *"Interrelating Nature, Humanity, and the Work of God: Some Issues for Future Reflection"* in **Zygon 27,** 4, 403-419.

Phillips, S. *"Changing of the Seasons"*. ABC News. **The Drum.** 21 March 2014. <abc.net.au>

Redd, N. T. *"Summer: The Warmest Season"*. **Live Science,** 19 June 2015.

Rich, J. *"The Gifts of the Autumn Years"*. The Blog, 21 November 2011. ,<huffingtonpost.com>

WINTER IS BROKEN!!

Winter is broken
Life returns abundantly
The sun brings healing!

Spring bursts out with joy
Sprite goddesses dance the new
Come season of change!

Join Persephony
In our break-out from hades
Buds tell old wood "LIVE"!!

Little boys run fast
Intense Berserker-style
Here in Ferney Creek!

They run exhubrance
Strength in the returning sun
Adonis reborn!

John Cranmer
September 2016

Theme focus: Earth/Early Spring

2. CELEBRATING EARTH AND WONDER IN EARLY SPRING...

"Earth is stardust-come-to-life, a magic cauldron
where the heart of the universe is being formed.
In me, the Earth and its creatures find their voices.
Through my eyes the stars look back on themselves in wonder.
I am the earth. This is my body"
(Daniel Martin)

In 2005 when I was on a Study Tour in England, I was fortunate enough to have a side-visit to 'Down House',
the country home of naturalist Charles Darwin and his family.
> Few properties can claim to have been as central to the life and work of its owner as this house.

I remember very well standing in his old study
and being engulfed by its history and its significance.
> For it was in that house and in that room that Darwin wrote his most famous book, **On the Origin of Species...** published in November 1859.

A book that stands as a wellspring for what we now call 'evolutionary biology'.

In the last paragraph of the book, Darwin wrote:
> "It is interesting to contemplate a tangled bank, clothed with many plants of many kinds, with birds singing on the bushes, with various insects flitting about, and with worms crawling through the damp earth, and to reflect that these elaborately constructed forms, so different from each other, and dependent upon each other in so complex a manner, have all been produced by laws acting around us."
> *(Darwin 2008:362)*

Interesting indeed...

For the debate it ignited not only led to the denial of the creation stories of the western religious tradition, it gave us
> the beginnings of an immensely richer, longer, more complex 'story', rooted not in "the history of a single tribe or a particular people",
>> but one "rooted in the sum of our knowledge
>>> of the universe itself".

A scientific 'doctrine of incarnation' as one person has described it, which suggests
> "that the universe itself is continually incarnating itself in microbes and maples, in humming birds and human beings, constantly inviting us to tease out the revelation contained in stars and atoms and every living thing."
> *(Bumbaugh 2003)*

Yes, a 'religious' story...
> that invites us to awe and wonder;
> that demands a vocabulary of reverence.

Prior to the rise of modern science, most people followed a literal interpretation of the biblical Genesis stories,
believing a flat earth was created
> about 4,000 years before the Middle Eastern itinerant peasant sage, Yeshu'a.

Or, if they followed Archbishop Ussher, it all started at 9.00am on 3 October 4004 BCE.[53]

Today, as I am sure you all know very well,
the most widely accepted modern estimate of the Earth's age - that third rock out from the Sun -
> is approximately 4.5+ billion years. While the observable universe - that whole

---

[53] Darwin believed the earth had to be about 400 million years old.

"complex, interrelated and interacting... matter-energy in space-time... of which humans are an integral part..."
(Gillette 2006:1)

is approximately 14 billion years old,
all let loose during an event called the Big Bang.

A misleading term really, in that there wasn't really
an explosion, but an expansion.

While careful not to over-estimate the reach and power of the natural sciences,
it is modern science that provides the foundation for this 'other' story.
It has been called 'the epic of evolution', 'the odyssey of life', 'the immense journey'
and most recently, geologian Thomas Berry named it, the 'Great Story'.

Sure, there was an outcry that scientific cold reason of facts without values was killing wonder, but for the most part science has become
the source rather than the nemesis of wonder.

And modern science is now saying

"[t]he history of the Universe is in every one of us. Every particle in our bodies has a multibillion-year past, every cell and every bodily organ has a multimillion-year past, and many of our ways of thinking have multithousand-year pasts."
(Primack & Abrams 2007:151)

Each of us is a collection of unfinished stories, within other stories. We are fully linked with our surroundings in time, space, matter/energy, and causality.
We do not live in straight lines.
We truly do exist in a web, a network, a maze...
We're genetic cousins to all living beings on earth.

Which is why a growing number of people around the world
are beginning to recognise that our modern life-style
and poll-driven politicians are
> harming other creatures,
>> diminishing the functioning of ecosystems, and
> altering global climate patterns.

Biology 101 teaches us that if amoebas are inserted into a drop of water infused with nutrients, their numbers will expand,
> until they become so densely populated
>> they deplete their essential nutrients, and die *en masse*.
>>> The drop of water again becomes uninhabited and sterile.

We humans are doing the same thing on planet Earth.

We are yet to learn from basic biology.
We are yet to learn that humans must cooperate with nature's processes,
> and if we can do that, then we can develop purposes
>> less likely to be frustrated by nature.

We are yet to learn that a debate between people who actually know stuff
> and people who just don't like what the experts have to say,
>> is not a 'balanced' debate. It's a waste of time.

And as Second Peoples connected to Seas and Oceans, we are yet to learn
> from the heritage of 60,000 years of interactions between First Peoples and Land.

There is no good reason to believe that taking nature to heart leaves a person with any fewer spiritual benefits
> than taking to heart the teachings of *super*naturalist traditions.

Neither do we need to think the sacred is a separate 'supernatural' sphere of life, driven by blinding-light revelations.

"Positing an incomprehensible, invisible, 'Other' does nothing to explain the incomprehensible 'other' that is palpably present, and that we actually encounter every second within and round us". *(Fleischman 2013:188)*

It could be said such sentiments are behind the hymn *"Seek Not Afar for Beauty"* found in the Unitarian Universalist hymn book **Singing the Living Tradition.**
> Its first verse claims this 'other':
>> Seek not afar for beauty; lo! it glows
>> in dew-wet grasses all about your feet;
>> in birds, in sunshine, childish faces sweet,
>> in stars and mountain summits topped with snows.

If we can go to special places, built by humans, which are designated as sacred, surely we can go to special places, shaped naturally, which are recognised as sacred...
> There is a strong monotheistic tradition of cutting down the sacred groves.
> What we need is to realise that to have a sense of sacred place is not tree worship
>> but rather the acknowledgment of the awesome,
>> and the overriding and the overwhelming.

There is also a need for all religious traditions to appreciate
that the primary sacred community is the universe itself,
and that every other community
> becomes sacred by participation in this primary community.

In moments of wonder we simultaneously contain a search for truth, an openness to reawakening, and a delight in what is.
> When we lose our sense of awe and wonder, we objectivise the Earth as a thing that can be used and abused at our consumeristic whim.

Yet during Winter we don't think much about any of these things.
It is only when Spring arrives and washes away the clouds of Winter fear,
> do we also see the Earth and "worms crawling..." and "new living things",
>
> as we begin to start again to 'grow' and 'bloom'.

Spring shows us that nature-kind and humankind are continually in relationship.
Spring reminds us and calls us forward to a 'new' religious sensitivity.
> To transcend the isolated self.
>
> To reconnect.
>
> To know ourselves to be at home.

So it is incumbent upon us to challenge the parochial and limited claims of traditional religions with the enlarging and enriching and reverent story
> that is our story and their story: the Universe Story.
>> From an attitude of reverence, we can then act with a morality
>>
>> that nurtures rather than destroys creation.

Religious naturalist and cell biologist Ursula Goodenough,
in her evocative book ***The Sacred Depths of Nature***, writes:
> "Once we have our feelings about Nature in place, then I believe that we can also find important ways to call ourselves Jews, or Muslims, or Taoists, or Hopi, or Hindus, or Christians, or Buddhists. Or some of each..."
>
> *(Goodenough 1998:173)*

With religious naturalism's acceptance of a diversity and plurality of theologies, perhaps you can see why religious naturalism is a perspective
> particularly acceptable to many Unitarian Universalists!

So I offer this gentle prod... It is time more people of whatever
persuasion, seriously thought about consciously and publicly
> *adopting* religious naturalism,
> *promoting* religious naturalism, and above all,
> *practising* religious naturalism.

ooOoo

Today a woman is planting flowers in her garden.
Her activity is more than a hobby, even more than a pleasure.
> She is digging, dirtying, straining, mulching and lugging,
> under the power of plants which do not yet even exist,
> but whose images have taken up residence in the atoms
> and cells within her imagination.

Weeks or months will elapse before her labour is fulfilled.
Patience and faith will sustain her until, under the majesty of
Earth's dominion,
> the unprepossessing little bulbs and seeds will explode into
> daffodils, tulips, irises, freesias, geraniums, pansies, daises
> and sunflowers.

A war will have been won by soft and coloured things.
The yellow eyes of asters, the purple tongues of irises, and the
crayola pansies
> have raised their banners above the turrets of Earth's soil
> to defy the dark cold space that pervades almost all of everything
> else.

(Adapted/Fleischman)

It is Spring.
If there were a heaven, the gods would abandon it
just for the chance to see this woman in her garden.
> Hosanna! Not in the highest, but right here. Right now.
> This.
>
> A Newer Testament. The gospel of the natural present
> moment.

Notes

Bumbaugh, D. *"Toward a Humanist Vocabulary of Reverence"*. Boulder International Humanist Institute, 22 February 2003.

Darwin, C. **On the Origin of Species by Means of Natural Selection**. London. Arcturus Publishing, 2008.

Fleischman, P. R. **Wonder: When and Why the World Appears Radiant**. Amherst. Small Batch Books, 2013.

Gillett, P. R. *"Theology of, by, and for Religious Naturalism"* in **Journal of Liberal Religion 6**, 1, 1-6. 2004.

Goodenough, U. **The Sacred Depths of Nature**. New York. Oxford University Press, 1998.

Martin, D. *"We are the Earth"* in Roberts, E. & E. Amidon. (eds). **Life Prayers from Around the World. 365 Prayers, Blessings, and Affirmations to Celebrate the Human Journey.** New York. HarperCollins, 1996.

Primack, J. R. & N. E. Abrams. **The View from the Center of the Universe: Discovering Our Extraordinary Place in the Cosmos.** New York. Riverhead Books, 2007.

Singing the Living Tradition. Boston. The Unitarian Universalist Association, 1993/2000.

Stone, J. A. *"On Listening to Indigenous Peoples and Neo-pagans: Obstacles to Appropriating the Old Ways"* in C. D. Hardwick, & D. A. Crosby (eds). **Pragmatism, Neo-Pragmatism, and Religion: Conversations with Richard Rorty.** New York. Peter Lang, 1997.

Tucker, M. E. & J. Grim (eds). **Thomas Berry: Selected Writings on the Earth Community.** Maryknoll. Orbis Books, 2014.

AND THE COMING OF SPRING

Here's to garden-awakenings
That are breaking-out from dormancy
In the frenetic embrace of returning sun
Opening-up the protective-spirals of new-life
With neo-nate buddings
Exploding from Mother-Wood
Spreading-fingers of becoming
Talking of what can be --- Again
In this place
Colour blazing-out
From ambient cocoon-waitings
Hope growing wings
And remembering what it can be

John Cranmer
November 2017

Theme focus: Humour

3. RELIGION AND THE NEED FOR HUMOUR IN OUR LIVES...

> "It is true that at least one medieval theologian, Petrus Cantor, is known to have asked during the course of his ruminations whether Christ ever laughed. Cantor was of the solemn opinion that he must have if he was truly [hu]man. What disturbs us today is that Cantor should ever have felt the need to ask the question."
> *(Harvey Cox)*

Scientists tell us, so that saying goes, that of all the creatures that live on earth, only humans have the gift of laughter.

Everyone loves a clown.
    A clown can do all the silly, ridiculous, nonsense things
    that we dare not do.

"The art of the clown, and it is a highly skilled art indeed, consists of doing the unreasonable in a reasonable way, or the reasonable in an unreasonable way. If the stool is too far from the piano, a clown isn't stupid if s/he moves the piano instead of the stool, he's funny." *(Nickerson 1969: 68)*

But in all seriousness not everyone knows **how** to laugh.
Many, it is said, only go through the motions of laughing.
    Their sense of humour is lacking,
    without which laughter is merely a muscular reflex.

Religion in general and Christianity in particular
has not for the most part appreciated the place of laughter
    in the human heart.

In fact, religion has often taken a pretty solemn and gloomy view of life.

At least that is the experience of many when religious attitudes are subjected to the so-called 'pub test'.

Religious people are often caricatured as dry and humourless. An article by Chris McGillion in the *Sydney Morning Herald* supports this view:

> "When humour surfaces in a church setting it seems somehow awkward if not unnatural and laughter erupts as a sense of relief more than an expression of genuine merriment." *(McGillion 2000)*

(Note: Back in 2000, on Pentecost Sunday, I had the following in my Sermon/Exploration...

Those who like to 'salt and pepper' everything with a biblical verse, are usually quick to point out
    the gospels speak of the Lord's tears,
    but do not record his smiles.

But 'holy laughter' in the foyer and aisles is a sign of a healthy congregation.

Like when the Sunday school teacher who told me about the time she told the parable of the Good Samaritan to her morning group.
    After telling the story, she asked why the priest
    didn't go over and help the injured man.

A little girl answered:
    "Because he saw that the man had already been robbed?"

You may appreciate this story, apocryphal of course!
The Prime Minister was making a public relations visit to a nursing home and came upon a wizened old man hobbling down the corridor.

*The PM took the man's hands in his own,
looked into his eyes, and said:
    "Sir, do you know who I am?"*

*The old man replied:
    "No. But if you ask one of the nurses, she'll tell you."*

*And then there was the teacher who asked her third-graders
to write about their personal heroes.*

*One little girl brought home her essay and showed it to her parents.
Her father was flattered to discover his daughter had chosen him
as her hero.
    "Why did you pick me?" he asked expectantly.*

*The little girl replied:
    "Because I couldn't spell Schwarzenegger."*

Do you hear the sound of laughter here?)

Way back when I was in my first Congregation (in the early 1970s),
hot out of theological seminary in Melbourne,
    my interest in communication saw me elected
    to the local Combined Churches Media Committee.

One one occasion, I was part of a team that wrote a 'religious' radio script which, in part, went something like this:

> "There is a man who seldom thinks about the church: but when he does he always has a vision, and in which he sees church people.
>
> "He shudders whenever he has this vision of church people for it is not only their appearance that frightens him. It is also their message.

"They tell him of all the things he dare not do, and he notices that everything they list is something he enjoys..."

And the reaction? Well, let's say it was interesting.
From the church-goers: criticism.
From the people 'on the street': agreement.

The Calvinist wing of the Reformation was not known for its exuberance or wit!

ooOoo

Always keen to push some theological boundaries,
Harvard Divinity School theologian Harvey Cox,
in his book ***The Feast of Fools***, suggests that the
"comic spirit is somehow closer to Christianity than is the tragic". *(Cox 1969:150)*

Then 18 years later, in April 1987, he published an article called "God's Last Laugh" in the journal <u>*Christianity and Crisis*</u>,
In it he suggested:
"God laughs, it seems, because God knows how [Easter] all turns out in the end."

Cox went on to say:

"On the Christian calendar Easter is a feast of gladness. Grief turns into jubilation. Bitter defeat becomes exuberant hope. Even those who walk in the valley of the shadow of death know they need fear no evil. But, without a trace of irreverence,
can we not also say there is something genuinely comic about Easter? Could it be God's hilarious answer to those who sported and derided God's prophet, who blindfolded and buffeted him, and who continue to hound and deprive God's children today?" *(Cox 1987)*

He had in mind, no doubt, the custom found in some Orthodox churches, where members meet in the church - usually on the Monday after Easter
>   (through to the following Saturday),
>   and called 'Bright Monday/Week' - for a feast and festival.

Games would be played. And there would be much laughter, dancing and joke telling.
Why? Because, they said, it was the most fitting way
>   to celebrate the 'big joke' God pulled on Satan
>   in the resurrection.

Now that tickles my fancy!
But it leaves us with the over-all question:
>   Why does laughter hold such a meager place in our religious life?

My reason for wanting to raise this question is simple.
Not just because all work, all seriousness, makes us dull and uninteresting people.
>   Clergy persons included!

Nor to have a go at so-called Fundamentalists, whom many believe have no sense of humour at all!
>   As another has suggested:

>   "the Christian fundamentalist has the awful fear that someone, somewhere, may be happy." *(H. L. Mencken)*

I raise it because a culture that causes people to be too serious all the time, and lacking in humour, can be a culture
>   in which progress and growth and compassion
>   can be lacking.

ooOoo

To say that comedy and humour are important
is in no way to detract from the seriousness of life.
> It is only to say that seriousness must be tempered with a sense of humour.

The person who can never laugh at herself/himself,
or even at their own pretensions, may easily become
> the reactionary who wants to destroy everything
>> that does not agree with her/his narrow focus of what is important.
> And 'twitter' us mad in the process!

Former minister at All Souls Church in New York, Walter Kring, suggested:

> "I would almost be willing to subscribe to the thesis that the most serious person, if he/she lacks a sense of humour, may be the most dangerous person in the world. This is particularly true in our day when so much power can be concentrated in the hands of so few".

In that sermon, Kring went on to make two suggestions
as to what he believed made up a balanced life:
> (i) Every life must have a serious purpose,
> (ii) We ought to temper this serious sense of purpose with good humour.

Very briefly, let me unpack some of his commentary.

The greatest people of our earth are those who have delved the deepest and who have found the most profound truths.
> While philosophers, scientists, and religious prophets have differed from each other,
>> they have all been seeking to find the basic nature of all things in all seriousness.

Thus they have highlighted the fact that the only way to truth is through experimentation.
> That through the process of testing
>> we shall eventually arrive at some generally accepted principles
>>> that will be felt to be true - unless
>>>> something more satisfactory is arrived at.

As people who take seriously 'progressive' religion, this should be particularly relevant to us.
Many people think of religion in terms of **dogma** - as law and answers,
> or what Bishop John Shelby Spong calls "killing certainties",
>> rather than as **search** - as questioning.

The latter are seekers.
They live the questions now.
> And who knows... perhaps someday in the future,
> gradually, and without ever noticing it,
>> they live their way into an answer.

David Felten and Jeff Procter-Murphy in their book *Living the Questions,* write about these 'christian' seekers:

> "These seekers are comfortable with ambiguity and understand that through difficulties, mistakes, and challenges, it's the journey that's important. It's what we learn along the way in relationship to the Divine and to one another that matters most."
> *(Felten & Procter-Murphy 2012:69)*

A 'serious purpose in life' must always be tempered with the realisation that no matter how inspired a leader,
or catechism, or book, or we may be,
> in the long run, both they and we are undoubtedly
>> not going to have the final answers to everything.

Yes... we all ought to be serious about life.
And we ought to search with all of our being
to find out what is true for us.
> We ought to use our brains to the best of our ability.
>> But we also ought to temper this seriousness,
>>> this serious sense of purpose, with good humour.

A well balanced life is going to be the life that truly understands the place of humour. Because laughter can help to herald in the dawn of human hope.
> Or at the very least, a hope about hope.

ooOoo

Let 'progressive/evolving' religion give long overdue recognition to the neglected gifts of humour, comedy, play, and laughter.
> May these 'gifts of grace' be used so the healing of human lives, for attaining balanced lives.

It would do us well to remember the words of American pastor and poet, Howard Thurman:

> "Don't ask yourself what the world needs. Ask yourself what makes you come alive, and go do that, because what the world needs is people who have come alive."
> *(Felten & Procter-Murphy 2012:70)*

The well balanced life is valuable, not because anyone says so,
but because in the long run
> it is the most satisfactory life.

And may the Monty Python film, *The Life of Brian,*
be aired for every theological/ministry student to see,
before graduation!
> For where it is real, laughter is the voice of faith.

Notes

Cox, H. *"God's Last Laugh"* in **Christianity and Crisis,** (6 April 1987).
– – – – –, **The Feast of Fools. A Theological Essay on Festivity and Fantasy.** Cambridge. Harvard University Press, 1969.
Felten, D. M. & J. Procter-Murphy. **Living the Questions. The Wisdom of Progressive Christianity.** New York. HarperOne, 2012.
Hyers, C. *"The House of Laughter"* in **Presbyterian Survey 80,** 3, (April 1990), 29 - 31.
Kring, W. D. *"The Need for Humor"*. A Sermon article. All Souls Church, New York City, (17 January 1971).
Nickerson, B. **Celebrate the Sun. A Heritage of Festivals Interpreted through the Art of Children from many Lands.** Philadelphia. J. B. Lippincott Co., 1969.
(Staff Writer) *"Christianity: A Laughing Matter"* in **Insights. The News/Magazine of the Uniting Church, NSW Synod.** (August 2002), 23-24.

Theme focus: Environment Day/Climate Change

4. 'ENVIRONMENT' IS MORE THAN OUR SUN, SAND AND SURF...

> "When you trek up a mountainside and pass over a ridge
> into a gorgeous vista of peaks bathed in the colours of sunset,
> and when later that night the stars spangle out over your tent and an
> alpine lake, reflecting back their own infinite mass,
> don't the words that come to mind
> feel strangely religious? Awe. Wonder. Beauty.
> Surely this, if nothing else, reassures us that
> the chasm between science and religion is not as wide
> as it all-too-often feels."
> *(Mary Evelyn Tucker, 2016)*

ooOoo

It was Christmas Eve in December 1968.
Apollo 8 was orbiting the moon, the American astronauts
   busy photographing possible landing sites
   for the missions that would follow.

> "On the fourth orbit, Commander Frank Borman decided to roll the craft away from the moon and tilt its windows toward the horizon – he needed a navigational fix. What he got, instead, was a sudden view of the earth, rising. "Oh my God," he said. "Here's the earth coming up." Crew member Bill Anders grabbed a camera and took the photograph that became the iconic image perhaps of all time."
> *(McKibben 2010:2)*

The space agency NASA gave the image
the code name AS8-14-2383
But we now know it as "Earthrise", a picture
> "of a blue-and-white marble floating amid the vast backdrop of space, set against the barren edge of the lifeless moon."
> *(McKibben 2010:2)*

This image, along with another of Earth from space,
called "Blue Marble", and taken by crew on board *Apollo 17* four years later,
> has appeared in TV mini-series,
> scientific publications and school text books,
> on greeting cards, a postage stamp, and advertising posters,
not to mention having their own pages on Wikipedia!

As the other *Apollo 8* Crew member, Jim Lovell, put it:

> "the earth… suddenly appeared as 'a grand oasis'."
> *(McKibben 2010:2)*

But author and environmental activist Bill McKibben has pointed out:

> "…we no longer live on that planet."
> *(McKibben 2010:2)*

Not that the world has ended.
It hasn't. You and me are still here – south east of the Wallace Line.
Earth is still a fragile web of interconnected and
> interdependent forces and domains of existence.

It is still the third rock out from the sun,
located in a galaxy called the 'Milky Way',

> "three-quarters water. Gravity still pertains; we're still earthlike."
> *(McKibben 2010:2)*

What has ended is the world **as we thought we knew it.**
That 'grand oasis' has changed in profound ways.

> "We imagine we still live back on that old planet, that the disturbances we see around us are the old random and freakish kind. But they are not. It's a different place. A different planet. It needs a new name." *(McKibben 2010:2)*

That 'different planet' has been brought about by global warming. The sudden surge in both greenhouse gases and global temperatures.

> And "a series of ominous feedback effects."
> *(McKibben 2010:20)*

ooOoo

Today is Environment Day.
So I reckon it is important for us to be reminded
    about the place we call Earth, and its environs.

Especially as many of us are lovers of 'sun, sand, and surf'.
That's why we live where we do!

In the world of **science**, the most widely accepted modern estimate of the Earth's age is approximately 4.5+ billion years. While the universe - that whole

> "complex, interrelated and interacting... matter-energy in space-time... of which humans are an integral part..." *(Gillette 2006:1)*

is approximately 14 billion years old.
Yes... 14 billion years in what is commonly (but mistakenly) called a 'Big Bang'.
Science also says the universe is very large indeed:
    perhaps consisting of 200 billion galaxies,
        each of which likely contains 100 billion stars.

So science is saying and has been saying, again and again:
> this 14 billion year old universe must be regarded **as a whole:**
> it is of **intrinsic value**, and each part,
>> galaxy,
>> organism,
>> individual atom,
> **participates** in that intrinsic value as each part or web,
> participates in this wonderful web of life.

Each part, rather than one species or organism
separating itself out as more important than the rest.

Karl Peters, Professor Emeritus of Philosophy and Religion, and former President of the Centre for Advanced Study of Religion and Science, writes:

> "Our planet, its life forms, and our own bodies contain the oxygen, nitrogen, carbon, iron, and other elements from earlier exploding stars. We are 'star stuff' – a part of the matter that was created earlier in the universe's history."
> *(Peters 2002:15)*

Turning to the world of **religion past** one story seems to have ruled. The popular belief that a mythical story in a larger collection of stories called *Genesis,*
> mandates the claim that humans are to dominate nature.

Further, the god G-o-d, in terms of this story,
is pictured as a sky-God.
Earth came into existence in October 4,004 BCE.
> And in turn, human beings, as bearers of God's image,
> are regarded essentially as 'souls' taking up
>> temporary residence in their earthly bodies.

This popular religious belief was seriously challenged by Lynn White, in what is now his famous 1967 article,
> *'The Historical Roots of our Ecological Crisis'.*

An article that was published several months before *Apollo 8* was orbiting the moon.
An article that some have suggested should be compared
> to Luther's "Ninety-five Theses." *(Santmire 2000:11)*

In that article White suggests
Christianity's attack on so-called pagan religion
> effectively stripped the natural world of any spiritual meaning.

Indeed, Christianity replaced the belief that the 'sacred' is in rivers and trees, with the doctrine that G-o-d is a disembodied spirit
> whose true residence is in heaven, not on earth.

The impact of this religious teaching has tended to empty the biosphere of any sense of G-o-d's presence in natural things.
> White writes:

> "By destroying pagan [religions], Christianity made it possible to exploit nature in a mood of indifference to the feelings of natural objects." *(White 1967)*

White goes on to suggest that, in this sense, the ecological crisis –
> global warming,
> irreversible ozone depletion, massive deforestation,
> higher than acceptable methane gas concentrations –
>> is fundamentally a spiritual crisis.

Jump forward thirty years and eco-theologian Thomas Berry challenges both religion and science.
> He identifies six ways humans have negatively placed themselves above the systems of the Earth. Three he attributes to religion:
>> (i) A belief in a transcendent, personal, monotheistic deity has removed the sacred dimension from nature/creation;

(ii) A belief in the spiritual nature of the human detaches us from the natural world;

(iii) A belief in 'redemption' from the natural encourages the attitude that caring for the Earth doesn't matter.

Perhaps all this is reason enough for us to share in
the celebration of Environment Day.

ooOoo

Hand-in-hand with matters concerning the environment
is the controversial issue of climate change.
 Faced with this issue, two questions need to be asked:
  (i) is the average global temperature increasing over time?
  (ii) if it is, is the increase caused by human interference, or is it attributable to natural sources?

Science, based on carefully analysed IPCC
(International Panel on Climate Change) reports, suggests:
  (i) there is no question that taken over the past 150 years, the average global temperature is slowly rising. The planet is getting warmer.
  (ii) again, scientists are nearly unanimous in relating the rising temperatures to an increase in pollution, "in particular due to the deforestation and the burning of fossil fuels." *(Gleiser 2016:158-163)*

As if to put a great big red line under all this…
a Draft Report (NCA4) of the Climate Change Report,
 prepared by scientists from 13 federal USA agencies
 was published in the *New York Times* (NYT) in August 2017.

In that Report, which was not fake news, the reality of climate change was expressed in clear tones...

> "Since NCA3 [National Climate Assessment3, 2014], stronger evidence has emerged for continuing, rapid, human-caused warming of the global atmosphere and ocean. This Report concludes that 'it is *extremely likely* that human influence has been the dominant cause of the observed warming since the mid-20th century. For the warming over the last century, there is no convincing alternative explanation supported by the extent of the observational evidence'."
> *(New York Times, 8/8/2017)*

It directly contradicted claims by President Trump[54] and members of his cabinet who continue to claim the human contribution to climate change is uncertain,
    and that the ability to predict the effects is limited.

The *NYT* reported the following day that the White House
and the Environmental Protection Agency
did not immediately return calls
    or respond to emails requesting comment!

Global warming "is not just another important issue that human beings need to deal with," writes theologian Sallie McFague, rather, it is the demand that we live differently.

> "We cannot solve it, deal with it, given our current anthropology. It... demands a paradigm shift in who we think we are. This is certainly not the only thing that is needed, but it is a central one,

---

[54] When Donald Trump pulled USA out of the Paris Accord on Climate Change, Bill McKibben wrote that reneging on Paris "is a stupid and reckless decision — our nation's dumbest act since launching the war in Iraq." But rather than being stupid and reckless in a typical Trumpian way, along the lines of his Twitter habits, for instance, the Paris withdrawal "amounts to a thorough repudiation of two of the civilizing forces on our planet: diplomacy and science." Thus, backing out of Paris not only "undercuts our civilization's chances of surviving global warming, but it also undercuts our civilization itself, since that civilization rests in large measure on those two forces." *(Quoted in Hogue 2017)*

for without it we cannot expect ourselves or others to undertake the radical behavioral change that is necessary to address our planetary crisis." *(McFague 2008:44)*

Business as usual is not an option!
    We have a responsibility to explore how our actions, thoughts, and being can support the 'web' of existence.

We humans are an expression and an extension of Earth's ongoing creativity.

"What is wrong with our culture is that it offers us an inaccurate conception of the self. It depicts the personal self as existing in competition with and in opposition to nature… We fail to realize that if we destroy our environment, we are destroying what is in fact our larger self." *(Freya Mathews 2007:290)*

ooOoo

Environment Day is important.
It's worth celebrating.

'Global warming' is **not** a future tense statement.
    It doesn't just concern our grandchildren.
    It concerns us.
It will not go away – despite the newspaper, radio and TV babblings of various 'shock-jocks'

Earth **is** a precious living habitat.
Earth **is** a fragile web of ecosystems. *(Habel 2009:43-46)*
    The universe is not a-part from us.
    Whatever we are, the universe is.

Religious naturalism's answers to questions about the environment and climate change are a kind of hopeful cosmic recipe for the functioning of all things.

But above all, religious naturalism says religion is human.
It is about us.

> "It is about manipulating our brains so that we might think, feel, and act in ways that are good for us, both individually and collectively." *(Rue 2005:1)*

As a religious naturalist I, along with others, claim that the sacred is fully present, hidden in the ordinary details of a life, any life.
    Expressed in 'creativity' and 'mystery', 'awe' and 'wonder'.

Allow yourself to be shaped by this creativity and this wonder.
But where to start?

Start with your own life.
Start with the fifty trillion cells of your body
    that are converting energy to make protein right now
    so you can read these words.

"We carry with us in our bodies the very environment in which we evolved", writes theologian David Bumbaugh.

> "The heat of our bodies is the heat of stars, tempered to the uses of life. The salt in our blood and in our tears is the salt of ancient oceans, encapsulated and carried with us, generation upon generation, into strange and distant places and circumstances. The past is not dead. It lives in us even now. The evolutionary universe, the ancient environment, the emergence of complex life – all are recapitulated in every moment of our existence…" *(Bumbaugh 2003)*

Or, if all that sounds too bio-historical…
    (i) start with the awareness that the body you are carrying around now won't be the body you'll be carrying around three, five, seven years from now.
        It will have completely rebuilt itself from the inside out.

> (ii) or start with your own irrepressible urge to be more,
>> or realise the fullness of your potential,
>>> or to fashion the best life possible from
>>>> your precious years on Earth. *(Sanguin 2012:138)*

Yet again, be as surprised as I was when I read Jerome Stone's comments:

> "If you want to know where the environment is, just feel yourself. That is where the environment is. The skin is not a wall around us. The skin, the lungs, the digestive tract are permeable membranes designed to let the environment in. So we ignore the environment at our peril." *(Stone 1998)*

Wow!
In me, the Earth and its creatures find their voices!

ooOoo

The miracle of life is not to walk on water.
The miracle of life is to walk on the green Earth in the present moment

> "in this our ecologically-ordered cosmos, pervaded as it is by glorious creativity."
> *(Kaufman 2004:127)*

Notes

Bumbaugh, D. *"Toward a Humanist Vocabulary of Reverence".* Delivered at the Boulder International Humanist Institute, Fourth Annual Symposium, Boulder, Colorado. 22 February 2003.
<http://www.uua.org/sites/live-new.uua.org/files/documents/bumbaughdavid/humanist_reverence.pdf>
Gillett, P. R. *"Theology Of, By, and For Religious Naturalism"* in **Journal of Liberal Religion 6**, 1, 2006, 1-6.
Gleiser, M. **The Simple Beauty of the Unexpected. A Natural Philosopher's Quest for Trout and the Meaning of Everything.** Lebanon. ForeEdge/ University Press of New England, 2016.
Habel, N. **An Inconvenient Text: Is a Green Reading of the Bible Possible?** Hindmarsh. ATF Press, 2009.
Hogue, M. *"Withdrawal from Paris Accord Reflects a 'Theopolitics' of American Exceptionalism"* in **Political Theology Today,** 29 June 2017. <www.politicaltheology.com> (Accessed August 2017).
Kaufman, G. D. **In the Beginning... Creativity.** Minneapolis. Fortress Press, 2004.
McFague, S. **A New Climate for Theology. God, the World, and Global Warming.** Minneapolis. Fortress Press, 2008.
McKibben, B. **Eaarth: Making a Life on a Tough New Planet.** Melbourne. Black Inc., 2010.
Peters, K. E. **Dancing with the Sacred. Evolution, Ecology, and God.** Pennsylvania. Trinity Press International, 2002.
Rue, L. **Religion Is Not About God.** New Brunswick. Rutgers University Press, 2005.
Sanguin, B. **The Advance of Love. Reading the Bible with an Evolutionary Heart.** Vancouver. Evans & Sanguin Publishing, 2012.
Santmire, H. P. **Nature Reborn: The Ecological and Cosmic Promise of Christian Theology,** Minneapolis. AugsburgFortress Press, 2000.
Stone, J. *"Inaugural Liberal Arts Lecture",* 1998, William Harper College, Chicago, quoted in M. S Hogue. **The Promise of Religious Naturalism.** Lanham: Rowman & Littlefield Publishers, 2010
Quote by Freya Mathews, Australian ecophilosopher and author, in M. Dowd. **Thank God for Evolution. How the Marriage of Science and Religion will Transform your Life and our World.** New York. Plume/Penguin Group, 2007.

Theme focus: Wisdom/Imagination

5. LEARNING TO BE MORE GENUINELY HUMAN...

"Wisdom ceases to be wisdom when it becomes too proud to weep, too grave to laugh, and too self-ful to seek other than itself"
(Kahlil Gibran)

What we believe about life makes a huge difference to us.

Irish theologian and poet, John O'Donohue,
observed in his best-selling book, ***Anam Cara:***

> "The imagination is the great friend of possibility. Where the imagination is awake and alive fact never hardens or closes but remains open, inviting you to new thresholds of possibility and creativity."
> *(O'Donohue 1997:183)*

Imagination is a vital and essential force. Yet it does not dictate.
  Imagination offers only the minimal
  in order to permit and encourage...
  to perceive a given situation
    in a completely new way.

In similar vein, wisdom is not special knowledge about something. It is a way of being, a way of inhabiting the world.
  For wisdom is the wherewithal to live in harmony with reality.

As an entry in ***Psychology Today*** records:
  Wise people generally share an optimism that life's problems can be solved and experience a certain amount of calm in facing difficult decisions.

If you fail to live in accord with the constraints and provisions of reality, then as religious naturalist Loyal Rue suggests, you are likely to perish, but

> "if you succeed, then you are likely to flourish. It seems obvious, then, that wisdom and inquiry go hand in hand: in order to acquire wisdom we must inquire about the nature and dynamics of reality." *(Rue 2012)*

Imagination and wisdom are universal human traits.

ooOoo

Throughout history, there have been countless iconic figures who are well known for possessing extraordinary wisdom and imagination.

While any selection of names will be contentious
– there are a plethora of religious traditions and their subdivisions –
    and many will not be considered or make this final list,
    I have taken the plunge and selected just two.

- Thich Nhat Hạnh - the Vietnamese Buddhist monk and peace activist, and
- Yeshu'a/Jesus of Nazareth - the peasant Palestinian sage.

However, I also admit that religious traditions are so complex that no one can claim a thorough knowledge of world religions,
    even of just a selected few.

To my first choice…
(i) ***Thich Nhat Hanh*** (1926 -) was born in Vietnam.
He now lives in Plum Village in the south of France.
    He entered a monastery at age 16, and was ordained a monk in 1949.

During the Vietnam War, in 1960, he went to the USA
to teach comparative religion at Princeton University,
> returning to Vietnam (when permitted) in 1963
>> 'to aid his fellow monks in their non-violent peace efforts.'

A world traveller/speaker/teacher, Thich coined the term 'Engaged Buddhism' - Buddhists who are seeking ways to apply the insights
> from meditation practice and dharma teachings
>> to situations of social, political, environmental, and economic injustice.

'Engaged Buddhism' has grown in popularity in the West.

He is now recognised as a *dharmacharya* (teacher) and as the spiritual head of the Tu Hieu Pagoda and associated monasteries.

As it has been observed by others, Thich's approach

> "has been to combine a variety of traditional Zen teachings with insights from other Mahayana Buddhist traditions, methods from Theravada Buddhism, and ideas from Western psychology to offer a modern light on meditation practice."

Some of Thich's notable 'western' students seeking his wisdom and insight include
> environmentalist and author Joanna Macy, and
> 'poet laureate of Deep Ecology' and Pulitzer Prize (Poetry) winner, Gary Snyder.

From his many short wisdom sayings (aphorisms) and teachings I have gathered three, thanks to others who have collected and stored them
> on various social media.

> "If you truly get in touch with a piece of carrot, you get in touch with the soil, the rain, the sunshine. You get in touch with Mother Earth and eating in such a way, you feel in touch with

true life, your roots, and that is meditation. If we chew every morsel of our food in that way we become grateful and when you are grateful, you are happy."

"We need enlightenment, not just individually but collectively, to save the planet. We need to awaken ourselves. We need to practice mindfulness if we want to have a future, if we want to save ourselves and the planet."

"We will be more successful in all our endeavors if we can let go of the habit of running all the time, and take little pauses to relax and re-center ourselves. And we'll also have a lot more joy in living."

And probably his most famous epigram: "Washing the Dishes to Wash the Dishes."[55]

These sayings show a teaching that is centred on the here and now.
They take seriously our place in the universe
and as part of the universe.
> Because our very existence is rooted in the fundamental processes of the universe itself.

And they are about 'mindfulness' – the habit of paying deep attention.[56]
> It is not a practice of distanced abstraction or dispassionate observation.
> It is instead the practice of selfless reflective abandonment
>> within the particularity of the here and now of the present.
>> *(Hogue 2010:181)*

---

[55] "That is, one trains oneself to keep one's consciousness alive to the present reality, to focus attention on the here and now, on the miracle of the soap and the water and the dishes and the process, rather than rushing through the chore mindlessly to get to whatever is next." *(Goodenough & Woodruff 2001:586)*

[56] "[Buddhist mindfulness… made popular in the West by Vietnamese Zen master Thich Nhat Hanh] is knowledge or wisdom that pulls the whole mind and heart of the knower toward a connection with the way things are in all their exciting particularity. You cannot be mindful and know things in a purely academic way; as you become mindful of something, your feelings and your behaviour toward it will not be untouched." *(Goodenough & Woodruff 2001:586)*

This deeper connection is stimulated in moments of wonder as we simultaneously contain a search for truth,
>an openness to reawakening, and a delight in what is.

Should you wish to pursue Thich's writings in more depth, a good place to start is his published *Essential Writings*, which brings together

> "snippets from [his] poetry, his Christian-Buddhist dialogues, his introductions to Buddhist sutras, and of course, his own well-spoken takes on core Buddhist ideas. If there is one word that sums up Nhat Hahn's Buddhism, it is "interbeing," the name he gave to his own monastic order. Being fully present in the moment is mindfulness, and interdependence tells how all things are intimately connected, the understanding of which encourages us to engage the world at every moment."
> *(Amazon Review: Brian Bruya)*

To my second choice…
(ii) **Yeshu'a/Jesus** was also a teacher of wisdom – a sage or wise man.
Through his parables and short sayings (aphorisms), he invited people to embrace wisdom
>so they could be agents of change and healing.

Jesus was Jewish. Probably born around the year 4 CE.
A peasant Galilean Jew to be exact, living under the oppressive rule of the Roman Empire.
>He never became a Christian. Not even the first Christian.
>He wrote nothing.
>He spoke Aramaic and very possibly some Greek.
>He lived and died in Palestine in the early years of the first century.

> "[And] although he is portrayed as accompanied by a small group of associates his career was essentially a solo act."
> *(Hedrick 2014:29)*

The world of Jesus' parables and short sayings is the fabric of daily life, Monday-to-Friday, in a Galilean village or family
> rather than an urban setting *(Scott 1989)* as seen
> in the writing of the bloke we call Paul.

The subjects of his parables were robbery on an isolated road, coins, a vineyard, day labourers, sheep, bread making, and wayward children.

His parables do not speak about the god G-o-d, neither does he develop a doctrine of G-o-d, proclaim his messiahship,
> predict his passion and death, depict a last judgment,
> commission the disciples to establish a church,
>> or picture supernatural beings or miracles. *(Funk 1994:105)*

However, despite all this and other affirmations, many preachers and scholars give this information no content, because as the historical Christian creeds reveal,
> a historical Jesus is not central to the teaching of the church,
> – since the 1930s called neo-orthodoxy.

"The Christian church historically is the body of those who 'confess' beliefs and dogmas, but the historical Jesus community is composed of those who 'profess' the credible and the sensible." *(Galston 2012:49)*

So, to his wisdom... expressed in short aphorisms and parables. Fictional concrete stories about the ordinary.
> With the majority lacking obvious religious motifs.

Some aphorisms...
> (i) No one pours new wine into old skins otherwise the wine will burst the skins and be lost along with the skins. But new wine is for fresh skins...
> (ii) Love your enemies...
> (iii) Be sly as snakes and simple as pigeons...

(iv) Consider how the lilies grow; they neither toil nor spin; yet I say to you not even Solomon in all his glory was arranged like one of these...

(v) If a blind person leads a blind person, both will fall into a pit...

And three parable outlines – again with help from scholar Charles Hedrick – will serve my purpose.

Two are from the 'canonical' gospels and one from the Thomas 'non-canonical' gospel.

(i) The Leaven *(Matthew 13:33; Luke 13:21)*
• Describes a woman making dough.
She disperses a small amount of fermenting agent (leaven) in a large amount of flour until it 'rises, that is until it became fermented dough.

(ii) A Man Going on a Journey (Mark 13:34)
• Describes preparations a person made with servants before leaving home on a journey

(iii) A Woman Carrying a Jar *(Thomas 97)*
• Portrays a woman on her way home with a jar full of meal.
The jar breaks and without her knowledge the meal is lost.

On these three parables, and after much discussion and debate, the Jesus Seminar – a collaboration of progressive scholars – voted/ concluded that:

(i) The Leaven = Red ("Jesus most likely said something like this")

(ii) The Journey = Grey ("Jesus probably didn't say it, but it contains some similar ideas")

(iii) The Jar = Pink ("Jesus may have said something like it")

Contemporary scholarship also shows the sayings of Jesus:
• do not point to him being an apocalyptic prophet announcing the end of the present world;
• there is no one final irrevocable 'meaning' to a saying for all time; and

- any wisdom in his sayings comes by pondering the force of his words in their first century context, then considering how they may apply to a totally different way of life in the twenty-first century. *(Hedrick 2014:83-85)*

Progressive/radical scholarship aside, what is clear is the wisdom contained in these Jesus aphorisms and parables is as an invitation – dare I even say 'subversive invitation' –
> to undermine the so-called common sense mentality of his listeners, in order to get them to see he is talking about an alternative 'this' world.

> "[The parables] exaggerate, poke fun at, employ irony, and other devices in order to reshape the lived world of his listeners. That world is a social world and is socially constructed, so [Jesus] employs the poetic fiction as a way of deforming the everyday world of Galileans." *(Funk 2006:62)*

As Loyal Rue has also said: religion is not about God. It is about us.

> "It is about manipulating our brains so that we might think, feel, and act in ways that are good for us, both individually and collectively." *(Rue 2006:1)*

ooOoo

Both wisdom and imagination invite us to embrace life in its many dimensions.
In joy and in sorrow.
In living and in dying.
In working and in resting.
In our going out and in our coming in.

Embracing all of life by growing seeds of wisdom in every encounter. Always open, always learning and imagining what life is really about
> while responding with integrity to whatever our future brings, working toward a fully humane world within the ecological constraints here on planet Earth.

Indeed, 'wisdom' is embedded in the biological name we have given ourselves, where the *sapiens* in *Homo sapiens* means "having wisdom".
> And the 'getting' of wisdom is needed in our own time and age as we encounter the contemporary cultural consumerist worldview
>> that equates happiness with material well being,
>> that regards our planet as a resource for our use and enjoyment, and
>> that measures progress materialistically by the GDP.
>
> *(Peters 2015)*

Former Harvard Divinity School theologian, Gordon Kaufman, offered these encouraging comments:

> "In the course of history, women and men have developed many diverse world views, many different conceptions of what life in the world is all about, of what the central human problems are and what solutions to them might be available… [They] seldom (if ever) understood themselves to be creating or constructing a picture of the world and of the human within the world… however, looking back at the many great and diverse cultural and religious traditions that have appeared in human history, all these conceptions and pictures seem best understood as the product of many generations of human imaginative creativity in face of the ultimate mystery that life is to us all. Out of and on the basis of such traditions of meaning, value, and truth, all women and men live." *(Kaufman 1996:58, 59)*

Therefore, echoing Kaufman, but with some additional notes by philosopher Jerome Stone (if I have understood them correctly), I offer these 'wisdom principles' for your consideration:
- (i) more than one religious tradition should be explored, especially in this pluralistic day and age;
- (ii) the counterpoint between divergent themes within a tradition should be explored rather than glossed over;
- (iii) such exploration needs to go beyond the 'official' interpretations stated by any tradition – boundaries need to be pushed, and where necessary, reconstructed;
- (iv) a sense of 'openness' or dialogue be encouraged... where both the self and the tradition is challenged to learn and to grow.

What we believe about life makes a huge difference to us.

Notes

Funk, R. W. *Funk of Parables. Collected Essays.* Edited by B. Brandon Scott. Santa Rosa. Polebridge Press, 2006.
– – – – -, **Jesus as Precursor.** Revised Edition. Sonoma. Polebridge Press, 1994.
Galston, D. **Embracing the Human Jesus. A Wisdom Path for Contemporary Christianity.** Salem. Polebridge Press, 2012.
Gibran, K. **Sand and Foam.** New York. Alfred A. Knopf, 1926/1954.
Goodenough, U. & P. Woodruff. *"Mindful Virtue, Mindful Reverence"* in **Zygon 36,** 4, (December 2001).
Hedrick, C. W. **The Wisdom of Jesus. Between the Sages of Israel and the Apostles of the Church.** Eugene. Cascade Books, 2014.
Hogue, M. S. **The Promise of Religious Naturalism.** Lanham. Rowman & Littlefields Publishers, 2010.
Kaufman, G. D. **God-Mystery-Diversity. Christian Theology in a Pluralistic World.** Minneapolis. Fortress Press, 1996.
O'Donohue, J. **Anam Cara. Spiritual Wisdom from the Celtic World.** London. Bantam Books, 1997.
Peters, K. E. *"Wisdom in Ancient and Contemporary Naturalism".* A Presentation to 'Seizing an Alternative: Towards an Ecological Civilization' Conference, Claremont, USA. 4-7 June 2015.
Rue, L. **Nature is Enough. Religious Naturalism and the Meaning of Life.** New York. State University of New York Press, 2012. (Kindle Edition).
– – – – -, **Religion is Not About God. How Spiritual Traditions Nurture Our Biological Nature, and What to Expect When They Fail.** New Brunswick. Rutgers University Press, 2006.
Scott, B. B. **Hear Then The Parable. A Commentary on the Parables of Jesus.** Minneapolis. Fortress Press, 1989.
Stone, J. *"Is Nature Enough? Yes"* in **Zygon 38,** 4, (December 2003) 795-796.
Thich Nhat Hạnh. Various Sayings… (< https://www.brainyquote.com/quotes/authors/t/thich_nhat_hanh.html>) Plus material from the Wikipedia entry under his name. (Accessed July and August 2017).

Theme: Autumn in the Southern Hemisphere

6. AUTUMN: THE SEASON OF LEAVES AND HARVEST...

> "You shall ask
> What good are dead leaves
> And I will tell you..."
> *(Nancy Wood)*

Let me tell you a story...
It is Autumn.
    We are in a town, strange to us.
    I open the window, then the shutters of our B&B guest room
        to look out over the town.

A burst of biting air suggests there was a white frost during the night. Over there, over the galvanised-iron roof tops,
    I see a church steeple.

It is Sunday.
We wrap up against the sharp morning air
    and venture into the deserted streets.

We peer into back gardens that have been well prepared
against the frost.
    Apple trees have been picked clean.
    Some plants have been hooded and blanketed against the cold.

It is cold and utterly quiet. Not a wind stirs
and no one in the town seems to be awake.

We round a corner and come upon a park,
a long terraced stretch that overlooks the roof tops
    and has a view into the river valley.

It is a park with a row of benches
interspersed with a long line of elm trees.
    They are a blazing yellow - each leaf like a giant, drooping glove.

The yellow is so shocking we halt in our steps to stare.
In the utter stillness we hear only the noise of the leaves falling.
    Plop. Plop. Plop-plop.

Up and down the row,
every tree is losing its leaves - right now in front of our eyes.
    The trees are raining down their leaves with steady determination.

Was it the frost that caused this event?
Or the first rays of sun?
    We stand in silence and watch.

Within half an hour, we see a whole row of golden trees
turn utterly bare before our eyes.
    Gaunt and grey, the empty branches reach at the sky.

At the foot of each tree is a perfect pile, yellow as sunlight.
A gift from the tree to its own roots.
    By the time the townsfolk wake, autumn is over.
    (Author Unknown)

ooOoo

Human beings are the creatures who celebrate.
We dance, sing, feast, fast and dramatise
    important moments and events in our lives.

Geologian Thomas Berry suggests:

> "Our experience of the universe finds festive expression in the great moments of seasonal transformation, such as the dark of winter, the exuberance of springtime, the warmth and brightness of summer, the lush abundance of autumn. These are the ever-renewing moments of celebration of the universe, moments when the universe is in some depth of communion with itself in the intimacy of all its components."
> *(Berry 2014: 179)*

Rituals are important.
Traditional rituals and festivals have ancient roots springing from very early ideas of life, the world, and the heavens.

As one author has suggested, ritual provides us
with a tool to think logically, emotionally, and ecologically.

> "[During rituals] we have the experience, unique in our culture, of neither *opposing* nature or *trying* to be in communion with nature; but of *finding* ourselves within nature, and that is the key to sustainable culture."
> *(LaChapelle 1984)*

There is a hymn in the Unitarian Universalist hymn book **Singing the Living Tradition,** written by Brian Wren, and called "We Are Not Our Own". Its first verse states:

> "We are not our own. Earth forms us,
> human leaves on nature's growing vine,
> fruit of many generations,
> seeds of life divine." *(#317, SLT)*

Most annual Autumn celebrations originated from seasonal changes in the lives of agricultural people.
> And they can be traced back through uncharted years to a time when human survival depended directly on natural events.

These festivals are usually related to the movement
of the earth, the sun, or the moon,
> and the changes these movements made in the lives of human beings whose behaviour was said to be governed by them. *(Nickerson 1969:x)*

For instance, in Celtic tradition, the year is divided into four periods of gateways, each heralded by a quarterly festival.
> Each period follows the lunar cycle that underlies the agricultural year.
> The Autumn quarter (August, September, October) was called Lughnasadh.
(Matthews 1995)

People looked forward anxiously to this time when

> "instead of surviving on the remnants of last year's harvest, they would 'be on the pig's back' with plenty." *(Matthews 1995:99)*

During this time, everyone was in the fields helping to bring in the grain. Work, yes. But also festivals and celebrations
> that marked a "deeper awareness of the marriage between the land and its people."

ooOoo

Today we celebrate Autumn. The season of leaves and harvest.
In Autumn, the interdependence of humans and the earth
> again comes into clear focus.

The garden's excess has been turned under the earth one last time.
We gather in some extra cans of rich, thick, soup.
> The wood pile has been stacked.
> The gas bottles filled and the electric blanket placed on the bed.

We turn indoors to build home fires, to turn inward...

Reflecting on this season, the Psalmist once wrote:

> "The earth has yielded its fruits;
> God, our God bless us,
> and may all the ends of the earth fear him." *(Psalm 67)*

While a Jewish scholar has said this about the season:
It should teach us two things:
> First, that we should respect equality and abhor inequality - the one being the source of justice, and the other of injustice.
>
> Second, that we should be grateful to God for having caused the earth to bring forth in abundance, for man and beast alike, not only for one meal, but until the coming of the next crop - all as a result of nature's love for its creatures.

But it is to the poets that we need to turn,
to sense the *feel* and poetic *beauty* of this season.
One such poet is Max Coots.

> "What use can old leaves be once down and turned to brittle and to brown?
>   For jumping piles if young enough?
>   To roll laughing in with stem ends poking sharp
>   and tickle bits wriggling down jacket necks...?
> "I suppose.
>
> "But most of all to be a consolation for adults, who,
> less convinced than younger ones of their powers to keep things as they are,
>   set a raked-up heap on fire and send a low smoke out of gray nostalgia for the nose.
>   To burn, not out of sheer resentment because they fell,
>   but just to see that final colour that only fire can show..."
> *(Extract. Coots 1971:50-51)*

ooOoo

Well, so much for the past. What of modern, 21st century, city life?
With all our computers and mobile phones,
> freeways,
> suburban shopping centres,
> plastic credit cards and
> packaged instant food...

How can we city folk celebrate Autumn that is traditionally based on a country harvest festival?

I mean to say... City people buy their milk in a cardboard or plastic carton! Country folk, less of them now I am told in media reports,
> rise early to milk the cows.

City people visit the local supermarket to spend their earnings! Country folk sell their stock at the local sale yards, to earn their income.

Of course, this is an over simplification
but perhaps it can serve to show how
> our society
> our culture
> our religious celebrations, have changed, or need to change.

Do we, as 21st century city folk, have an Autumn festival to celebrate? We certainly have enough leaves in our Australian cities!

So my answer is 'yes!' even if that response comes with two conditions:
- an ecological concern for our world must be taken with radical seriousness, and
- for the sake of future generations, our generation is called upon to lament its self-indulgent ways.

When all the conditions are right,
life, growth, and reproduction, appears.

That there **is** a reality that lures life forth and forward
and strives against the forces of inertia and death...
> We can celebrate this.

When all the conditions are right,
beauty, truth and a concern for others, is alive.

That there **is** a creativity that lures forth honesty and love
and strives against the retreat to merely habitual behaviour...
> We can celebrate this.

And for some they can name this process, this creativity, G-o-d.

ooOoo

Now, for something a bit more personal...
In the earlier stages of life it is all about making it in the 'real' world. For those who are in the 35 - 45 year bracket, that is, preceding one's personal 'autumn' years,
> they are heavily engaged in building a career,
> gaining knowledge and experience,
> working hard to earn money, and
> provide a living for one's self and one's family.

In short it is about achieving, accomplishing,
accumulating or surviving.

But in later life, as our personal 'autumn' approaches, the focus shifts. Our orientation becomes more inward.
> Much of the 'doing part' of life begins to dissipate,
> or at least to slow down. And reflect...

> "If I were twice as old as I am now, I could tell you
>   how it was when I was just a boy,
> And you would smile indulgently and maybe even listen,
>   for old men are supposed to rummage through what's been..."

Often it is at this personal 'autumn' stage of life we can,
perhaps for the first time in too many years,
begin to note the words of the poet:

> "We deceive ourselves with clocks and calendars
> and dates on graves.
> Lived time is never by numbers…" *(Coots 1971:11, 18)*

Notes

Berry, T. *"Loneliness and Presence"* in Evening Thoughts, in M. E Tucker & J. Grim. (eds). **Thomas Berry: Selected Writings on the Earth Community.** New York. Orbis Books, 2014

Coots, M. **Seasons of the Self.** Nashville. Abingdon, 1971.

LaChapelle, M. D. *"Ritual is Essential. Seeing Ritual and Ceremony as Sophisticated Social and Spiritual Technology"* in In Context, 5, (Spring 1984), 39.

Matthews, C. **The Celtic Book of Days. A Celebration of Celtic Wisdom.** New Alresford. Godsfield Press, 1995.

Nickerson, B. **Celebrate the Sun. A Heritage of Festivals Interpreted Through the Art of Children from Many Lands.** Philadelphia. J. B. Lippincott Co., 1969.

Wood, N. *"You shall ask"* in Roberts, E. & E. Amidon. (eds). **Life Prayers from Around the World. 365 Prayers, Blessings, and Affirmations to Celebrate the Human Journey.** New York. HarperCollins, 1996.

EXPLORING A QUIETNESS OF TREES

Enticed into a place of dynamic silence
to walk within this presence of trees
with eyes non-focussed
called to the contemplation of in-scape

Feel here this anticipatory-hush
a holding of breath a coming to be
a birthing of the new

Here is a settledness
slowly gestating
marking seasons
of growth of loss
of consolidation

Intimacy of awareness
just beyond the reach
of questing fingers
of searching minds
of intricate imaginings

Rustling leaves
tinkling water
zephyr-breezes amongst bird-wings

Silence and sound organically intertwined

Presence fleetingly observed
through the corners of our eyes

Attempt to look them in the face
and they are --- gone!!

John Cranmer
February 2015

Theme focus: G-o-d/Jesus

7. SOME STUFF I HAVE PICKED UP ALONG THE WAY ABOUT JESUS AND G-O-D AND THE WORLD...

> "Whatever conclusion one might come to about Jesus,
> it must be a possible Jesus and not an incredible one."
> *(David Galston)*

The gospel storyteller called John is a fine storyteller.
He tells his stories and presents his arguments with passion and vivid imagery.
    And he does all this many, many years
        after the time when the events are supposed to have happened.

Yet on other occasions his writing can be dense and difficult to understand. The gospel story we heard this morning *(John 3:14-21)* is, I reckon,
    one of those occasions,
    despite it containing a familiar text.

Especially if you can remember it in the King James language...
(So I might quote it correctly I have had to get out my late parents' Bible...)

> 'For God so loved the world that he gave his only begotten Son,
> that whosoever believeth in him should not perish,
> but have everlasting life.' *(John 3:16, KJV)*

Now when we hear this particular story from John
we need to note that the traditional interpretation
      is on Jesus as 'the way, the only way', to the god G-o-d.

But when we go beyond the literal,
the emphasis is on the nature of G-o-d
> as reflected in the faith and teaching of Jesus of Nazareth.

So, what can we make of this 'shift'? This dichotomy?

The traditional emphasis is based on a belief
that the human Jesus is speaking these words in this story.
> But many scholars now claim this is not the case.
> These words are the words of the storyteller John, not Jesus.

The traditional emphasis has also resulted in a form of Jesus idolatry, where, in fundamentalist Christianity, for example,
> Jesus is portrayed as the god G-o-d
> and worshipped as though he were the god G-o-d.

As a result, this emphasis has led some to demand
agreement with this claim is a primary test of one's orthodoxy.

And as if to make everything OK and acceptable,
such groups usually argue this really means you have to
> 'accept the Nicene Creed'... whatever 'accept' may mean!

For others, it has led to a powerful religious exclusiveness.
And an exclusiveness that has been quite destructive
> in the relationships between Christians
>> and followers of other faith traditions,
>>> not to mention destructive of the lives of countless human beings.

With some very broad strokes, let me offer a few brief comments about Jesus and G-o-d I have picked up along the way.

(i) Although G-o-d is not a supernatural being or quasi-person,
 – often called substantive thinking – what G-o-d is remains a genuine mystery.

Even *mysteria poetica* as now being suggested
by some progressive biblical scholars.
> Both these words hold the sense of 'making' or 'doing'.
> *(Galston 2017)*

So, for instance, if we think of G-o-d as 'creativity', creativity as 'G-o-d' – the process or random emerging of the new, the novel, and the selecting of certain new emergences to continue –
> then G-o-d is always and everywhere active:
>> from the Big Bang through the cosmic expansion into galaxies;
>> through the appearance of life on planet Earth
>>> and its evolution into countless forms; and
>> including human cultural activity
>>> and self-conscious deliberations.

"This is religious naturalism," suggests Jerome Stone in another context,

> "Insofar as the divine power is located creatively and redemptively within the world. It is a rejection of fossilised institutions and overbearing individual egotism."
> *(Stone 1995:440)*

Insofar as we live our lives in such a way as to allow both random variation and natural selection to occur

> "and inso far as we promote this interaction within the larger systems of the society and physical universe to which we belong, we fulfil the divine image within us and are worthy of being called 'children of God'." *(Peters 1974:124)*

(ii) Jesus is truly human, bone of our bone and flesh of our flesh, living a human life under the same conditions any one of us faces.
> He is not a visitor from elsewhere,
>> sent to the world by a god 'out there'.

In recent years, particularly in critical biblical scholarship,
there has been less talk about a 'divine' Jesus
> resulting in Jesus been given a 'demotion'.

Such a demotion of Jesus has kept Jesus' value
as a centrally exemplary human being,
> often compared with the Buddha, Mohammed or Moses.

In other words, Jesus has remained a central figure for the faith of progressive Christians, while becoming more human than divine. *(Taussig 2006:27)*

(iii) Jesus is that one in whom the early Jesus Movement saw
G-o-d's creativity presence with a decisive intensity.
And this presentness brought about newness of life for humanity.
To expand life. Not escape life.

Richard Holloway, the retired Bishop of Edinburgh, writes:

> "It is a question of whether we emphasise the sheer gifted joy of being alive or the undoubted fact that we are always capable of destroying our own peace and polluting our own habitation... Grace and the celebration of life, rather than dread and the fear of death, becomes the motivators of life and action."
> *(Holloway 2001:241)*

Jesus' theology was a theology of life rather than a theology of death.

(iv) The distinctive voice of Jesus can be found
in the fragments known as sayings, parables and aphorisms.
> Especially in the stories called parables, as they offer
>> a glimpsed alternative...
>> a hint of new possibility...
>> a stretch of the imagination.

Professor of religious studies, Charles Hedrick, suggests it appears Jesus was

> "a parsimonious talker. He wasn't given to long-winded speeches. His discourses basically took three forms: short quips, brief summaries, and rather secular stories." *(Hedrick 2017:4)*

Secular stories… Performance stories… where the god G-o-d is never really mentioned but rather is implied as part of the work the parable performs.

And (v) by the time of John, near the end of the 1st century, some 65 -70 years or so after the death of Jesus/Yeshu'a,
> there had been a significant change in thinking by the Jesus Movement.

Away from the wisdom **teachings** of a human, secular sage, to the **person**, and indeed the worship of, the person Jesus as 'Divine Son of God'.
> And that was a momentous switch!

Now, moving forward in a great leap to our current times…
Progressive thinking distinguishes between the historical Jesus (pre-Easter Jesus) who lived in a particular time and place,
and the mythical Christ (post-Easter Christ).
> This distinction has been paraphrased further in some biblical studies as:
>> the 'gospel of Jesus' versus the 'gospel of Christ'.

In reality, the historical Jesus is 'smothered' by superimposing the heavenly figure of the Christ myth on him.
> Jesus is displaced by the Christ as the so-called Apostles' Creed makes evident…
>> Nothing between his birth and death appears to be essential to his mission or to the faith of the church.

ooOoo

With similar broad strokes, let me also offer a few very brief comments about the world, I have also picked up along the way.

The term 'global village' is one that is often used nowadays to describe the kind of world in which we live.

Indeed it is now not unexpected that we could:
> purchase a German car made in Mexico,
> or own a Japanese-named microwave built in Korea,
>> by an aircraft manufacturer.

Never before have so many people with so many different belief systems, values, and styles of life
> become aware of one another.

But for many this new awareness has also brought with it a realisation of all that divides:
> different cultural systems,
> different religious traditions
> different attitudes towards promoting a sustainable universe.

Some time ago I picked up this story from the Catholic e-zine publication called ***Eureka Street:***

> "On Smith Street, an archetypal inner suburban street, rain fell on the corrugated supermarket veranda.
>
> "It was about a month after the sub-prime market collapsed. Underneath the verandah the regulars,
>> and others in need of a meal,
>> sipped hot soup or munched on sausages.
>
> "From behind the BBQ I asked one of the regulars if he had collected any aluminium cans in the past week.
>> 'No, not this week.' He glanced up.
>> 'The rain?' I suggested.

'Nup,' interjected another bloke, 'no point anymore.'
'Yeah,' continued the first, 'scrap dealer says China doesn't want aluminium now.'

"We were at a St Vinnies' soup van on a street that brings together an eclectic mix of bohemians, disadvantaged and homeless.
>It is a hub for drug users, residents of surrounding
>>housing commission flats, as well as a large Aboriginal community.

"A number of the van's regular clients collect aluminium cans. They then sell them on to a scrap dealer
>who has them melted for recycling.

"This is by no means the easiest way to make a buck...
[But] the financial crisis meant that the demand
for raw materials dried up.
>So the dealer halved the price he offered for the cans.

"In so much of the debate surrounding the recent market collapses and economic stagnation, 'Wall Street' and 'Main Street'
>have been cast at polarities.

"This belies the more complex reality of the connection between the financial centres of the world
>and my mates on Smith Street." *(Butler. Eureka Street/2.09)*

The old King James words: God so loved **the world** does seem to imply that if it is to be an age of life and light, we will all need to:
- acknowledge an interconnectedness with people of all races, ethnicity's and cultures; and
- rejoice in those diversities as gifts to humanity and the wider web of life, without discrimination.

In a radically interconnected universe,
the smallest difference can lead to enormous change.
>   We literally cannot tell what difference
>   our smallest act will make.

When the price of aluminium cans goes down,
the poor are directly affected!

ooOoo

Now I guess all this sounds pretty heavy... Even too theological. Ideal material for yawns and reading the weekly Notices during sermons!
>   So my apologies to those who think
>   attending 'church' should mean you don't have to think!

But my own theological honesty requires me to claim:
>   • It is in Jesus-as-human that humans can see
>   Creativity G-o-d dancing within and among us,
>> not as the Holy Stranger,
>> but as the Familiar Sacred.

>   • It is in Creativity G-o-d that we can live in harmony
>   with others and with the earth,
>> even as we love our human selves.

>   • It is through the results of scientific cosmology,
>   evolutionary biology, and human history
>> that a new world narrative can be written and told.

May we yet be blessed in that claim.
Even as we continue to grow in knowledge and connectedness,
>   so the planet that is our home in the universe
>> will also continue to grow and flourish.

I reckon Don Cupitt's comment is helpful:

"the task of religion is to give us the courage and strength to commit ourselves wholeheartedly to life." *(Cupitt 2008)*

Notes

Butler, J. *"The Crash of the Can Market"* in **Eureka Street 19**, 3. 3 February 2009.
Cupitt, D. **Above Us Only Sky. The Religion of Ordinary Life.** Santa Rosa. Polebridge Press, 2008.
Galston, D. *"Mysteria Poetica: Some Reflection of the God Question".* Westar Institute Ethics & Early Christianity Blog. 28 July 2017.
Funk, R. W. **A Credible Jesus. Fragments of a Vision.** Santa Rosa. Polebridge Press, 2002.
Galston, D. **Embracing the Human Jesus. A Wisdom Path for Contemporary Christianity.** Salem. Polebridge Press, 2012.
Hedrick, C. W. *"The Church's Gospel and the Idiom of Jesus"* in **The Fourth R 30,** 4, (July-August 2017), 3-7, 26.
Holloway, R. **Doubts and Loves. What is Left of Christianity.** Edinburgh. Canongate Books, 2001.
Peters, K. E. **Dancing with the Sacred. Evolution, Ecology, and God.** Harrisburg. Trinity International Press, 2002.
– – – – -, *"The Image of God as a Model for Humanization"* in **Zygon 9,** 2, (June 1974), 98-125.
Scott, B. B. (ed) **Jesus Reconsidered. Scholarship in the Public Eye.** Santa Rosa. Polebridge Press, 2007.
Stone, J. *"Bernard Meland on the New Formative Imagery of Our Time"* in **Zygon 30,** 3, (September 1995), 435-449.
Taussig, H. **A New Spiritual Home. Progressive Christianity at the Grass Roots.** Santa Rosa. Polebridge Press, 2006.

Theme focus: Blessing of Animals

8. OF DOGS AND CATS AND... : TOWARDS A LIFE-CENTERED RELIGION...

> "To be life-centered is to be respectful of both
> life and environment."
> *(Jay McDaniel)*

This comment has been offered by American process theologian, Jay McDaniel, in his book ***Of God and Pelicans.***

McDaniel is concerned that we need to shape
a new way of thinking about religion and the god G-o-d –
> a theology that lives out of a sense of kinship with all life,
> not just human life alone.

He says:

> "An inclusive life-centeredness is needed because 'the least of these' now include animals subjected to cruel treatment in factory farms and scientific laboratories, endangered and extinct species whose habitats have been disrupted by direct and indirect exploitation, and the Earth itself, with its shrinking forests, eroded topsoils, encroaching deserts, contaminated waterways, polluted atmosphere and depleted ozone layer".
> *(McDaniel 1989)*

ooOoo

Within our religious tradition, there is one person who stands out
as an advocate of this kind of thinking... Francis of Assisi.
    Il Poverello, "the little poor man", as Francis was called,
        was born in Assisi, Italy, in 1182,
            the son of wealthy merchant parents.

Tradition has it he grew up as a cheerful and bright young man.
But in spite of his love of luxury and pranks,
    he saw many inconsistencies in and around him.
He knew there had to be something better.

During recuperation from a long illness, when he was about twenty-two years of age, he turned to reading the Bible to pass the time.
    Thus, he was exposed to the character and teachings
    of the Galilean peasant sage, Yeshu'a/Jesus.

He was particularly attracted by what he read in Matthew 11:28...

    "Come to me all you who are weary and heavy laden, and I will give you rest."

Francis acknowledged he needed to change his priorities.

His party mates started seeing less and less of him.
And with his loss of enthusiasm for making money,
    his enraged father kicked him out of home...
        'that dreamer, is no son of mine'.

People began to take him a bit more seriously as time went on.
    One by one, other young men began to seek him out privately.
    Now they were changing too.

When the group numbered twelve, they journeyed to Rome
and received verbal permission to become a monastic community.
    Later, to be known as the Franciscans, the Order
    was destined for the next seven centuries

to extend its influence to every part of the globe,
establishing itself within both Catholic and Protestant traditions.

Tradition says Francis died on 4 October 1226,
which is why we remember him on that October weekend.
    And while he was probably the first to begin shaping a life-centered theology, he is also popularly known for a Christmas event he fostered.

Tradition also says, following a visit to Bethlehem in the year 1220 CE, Francis returned to his own village and decided to recreate that experience.
    He built a manger in a cave,
        placed a stone image of the baby Jesus in it
        and surrounded it with real animals.

And it was reported that the atmosphere was so intense,
it was possible to believe that you were standing at the actual birth.
    From then on, nativity scenes,
        using large painted wooden figures of the Holy Family,
            became exceedingly popular.

oo0oo

In today's health circles, closeness with animals is widely promoted as being good for human health.

That closeness provides:
    love and companionship,
    reduces stress, and
    improves state of mind and body.

In many cities, "Pets as Therapy" programs have been established. But long before these current programs became popular
>a group of people with a love of horses,
>>began in 1963 in Brisbane, Australia, to work with disabled children.

This group is now called *Riding for Disabled* (RDA), an international association made famous through Mary Small's popular book, **And Alice Did The Walking.**
>My spouse was for many years an accredited Coach with RDA.

Riding for Disabled programs assist in rehabilitation and therapy. So it is much more than offering pony rides to children and adults.

Susan Cusack, a former National Executive Director of RDA says:

>"Once riders with disabilities are on the horse, the movement of the horse is very good for improving their coordination and balance. And in some cases, with some disabilities, it helps the muscles to get stronger".

She says there is a psychological benefit for many of the riders in being mobile and being able to go faster than they normally can
>with their crutches or wheelchairs.

>"Often it also works over into their educational program and into the development of life skills. Really the horse is the king, the centre piece, of the whole program. Children can do exercises with a physiotherapist and get very bored and very tired of it and not enjoy it very much. But when they do the same things on a horse in an outdoor context, it's totally different."

ooOoo

Jay McDaniel is concerned that as progressive Christians we need to shape a new thinking about religion, G-o-d and the world.
> A theology if you will, that lives out of a sense of kinship with all life, not just human life alone.

Not just human life... and not just Christianity.
Buddhism, and related eastern religions also tell us
to extend our kinship
> to all beings, not only human beings.

Which can raise some tough questions for many of us who also have to live with plenty of mosquitoes from the nearby wetlands,
> and who love to share the 'bliss' of a summer's evening!

One overseas colleague, in raising a similar question about insects in his home, writes:

> "They too are on the frontier of the universe – the frontier of time. Just as it has taken fourteen billion years to bring each of us humans into being, so it has taken the same time, the same galaxy and star formations, the same supernovae creating the elements, the same transformation from molecules to living organisms, and the same Darwinian evolution to bring insects such as flies, ants, and wasps into being."

So he has developed an insect-friendly technology:
> a square plastic food storage container and a stiff piece of paper.

When an insect lands on a window of wall

> "I gently put the plastic container over it... Next I slide the stiff paper behind the insect and over the cover of the container. Then I transport my fellow earth creature outside... and release them to continue their journeys on the frontier of time in their trajectories of the history of our universe. In doing this I try to live out a story of friendship with all beings. A story of

supporting life as much as I can." *(Peters 2006)*
A simple 'Blessing of the Pets' service
might not seem much on the surface.
Maybe even thought by some as just a gimmick or waste of time.
> But as I have been reminded by another, such a service confirms:

(i) religion has to do with life on this earth. Divinity is not something far from us, but it is here and now. All life is sacred if we have eyes to see, ears to hear, minds to understand, and hearts that can feel;

(ii) humans are but one of many life forms, and we find our place on earth as part of a larger organic wholeness of things. The other creatures of the earth were not created for us, but we are part of them, and we belong to them as they belong to us in one larger totality of existence;

(iii) the ethics of religion – the way we treat others – has to do, not simply with how we treat other humans, but with how we relate to all living creatures, to all life forms, and to the earth itself, and

(iv) religion has to do with the body and not only the mind and spirit. Religion is related to the physical world and to the senses, not just the spiritual or the realm of imagination. *(Bode 2001)*

And I would add another... such a service/Liturgy is a first step towards shaping a life-centered theology.
> A life-centered theology which is open
> - to future hopes rather than past achievements, and
> - to a future where there is love and justice among people, harmony with nature, and communion with the sacred...

"Its great wings outstretched, the brown pelican spirals in the thermal air. Scarcely a flicker of those magnificent wings is required for it to soar further and further aloft. Finally reaching an apogee of the spiral, it gently banks and slowly descends, only to be uplifted again in its circling flight... For me, at that

moment, this pelican's flight is a compelling symbol of the numinous powers, presences, and wonders of the natural order to which we both miraculously belong."
(Donald Crosby)

Notes

Bode, B. A. *"Blessing of Animals"* Service. Hope Unitarian Church. 30 September 2001.
Crosby, D. **More Than Discourse: Symbolic Expressions of Naturalistic Faith.** New York. SUNY Press, 2015.
McDaniel, J. B. **Of God and Pelicans. A Theology of Reverence for Life.** Louisville. Westminster/John Knox Press, 1989.
Peters, K. E. *"On the Frontier of Time"*. A Sermon, Unitarian Society of Hartford, 14 August 2006.
Sanguin, B. **Darwin, Divinity, and the Dance of the Cosmos. An Ecological Christianity.** Kelowna. CopperHouse/Wood Lake Publishing, 2007.

MISSIE

(Reflection on a Wounded Healer)

She places her labrador head
Expectantly on your knee
Licks your fingers
And pushes her
Anorexic rottweiler body
As close as she can to you
Forming her contours
Into the length of your leg
As you sit on the kitchen chair
In the place where she belongs

This with an intensity
Edging the anxious
Her eyes deep wells of sadness
Searching for acceptance

But be careful not to move
Too sharply too unexpectedly
She has an underlying fragility
Quite common for such rescue dogs
Taken from places of strong depredation
Knowing what male hands can do

Yet she who at core being
So needs acceptance and healing
Is able out of her woundedness
To be there for those walking
Their own edge of fragility
An innate struggle that calls out strength
Through the bonding of unconditional love

John Cranmer
May 2017

Theme focus: Evolution/Darwin

9. THE LIBERATION AND NOVELTY OF 'EVOLUTIONARY' LIFE...

> "We are the universe in the form of a human."
> *(Thomas Berry)*

Things that are new and different and perhaps a little dangerous always cause a stir, at least for a while.

And people who have the courage to be different,
and more especially those who carry a hint of danger,
> are always the source of excitement and interest.

Two readings stand in sharp contrast to each other.
> One from the biblical world *(Mark 1:40-45)* of the 1st century CE, shaped by thinking hundreds of years old.
> One from the natural science world (from **On the Origins of Species**) of the 19th century CE.

Both have had an impact on the way many religious people think today.
Different. Dangerous.
> So let's explore just some of that impact, now.

ooOoo

Leprosy, in the time of Jesus, was sometimes regarded as divine punishment for sin. It embraced a wide range of disorders, including
> rashes,
> acne,
> eczema
> and other forms of dermatitis.

It made people 'unclean'. Dirty.
And when you were dirty, so the claim went, you offended God's standards.
> Indeed, there was an explicit connection between
> being clean and being holy.

And when you were 'unclean', you weren't 'holy'!

This was the culture into which Yeshu'a / Jesus was born.
This was the culture that was learned and cultivated.

In a string of stories commenced a week or two back,
Mark's Jesus is confronted with a series of 'unclean' people,
> usually captured by 'unclean' spirits.

As a modern 21st century person, who both accepts and relies on modern medical science, I find it very difficult to believe in the existence
> of unclean spirits or demons, even though I agree
> there are some moderns as there were ancient folk, who do.

So what are we to make of this and other stories?
Following the thoughts of some scholars whom I trust,
> whether Jesus was or was not a genuine shaman

> > "or whether he simply embraced the company of the unclean, the meaning of his memory is the same: in Jesus we have come to know a God who renders impotent the power of dirt to keep the unclean outside the human community."
> > *(Patterson 2002:210)*

And I come to this conclusion as a result of modern critical biblical study, established some 300 years ago, and given exposure
> in the late 20th century through the pioneering work
> of the Westar Institute and its founder, Robert W. Funk.

That's the first thing I want to share.

ooOoo

The second is... today is Evolution Sunday and once again
I have decided to be a signatory to *The Clergy Letter*, now in several variations,
> that supports the validity and merit of evolutionary science as

> "a foundational scientific truth, one that has stood up to rigorous scrutiny and upon which much of human knowledge and achievement rests. To reject this truth or to treat it as 'one theory among others' is to deliberately embrace scientific ignorance and transmit such ignorance to our children."
> *(UUA Clergy Letter. www.evolutionweekend.org).*

And while the term 'evolution' was in use dating from 1647, and there were certainly others with similar views, it is English-born Charles Darwin ((1809-1882)
> who is now recognised as the 'founder' of the theory of evolution, leading the way to the modern study of
>> genetics and molecular biology.

Charles Darwin,
raised in a Unitarian household, attended High Street Unitarian Church in Shrewsbury,
> but was taken by his father to the Church of England because Unitarians could not attend university.

Charles Darwin,
whose father once said of him:

> "You care for nothing but shooting, dogs, and rat-catching, and you will be a disgrace to yourself and all your family." *(Wilson 1998:16)*

Charles Darwin,
who first studied medicine at Edinburgh University, but left after only 18 months

> "partly because of the barbarity of 19th century surgery long before the days of anaesthetics" *(Wilson 1998:18)*,

and went to Christ's College, Cambridge, because his father determined that he should 'become a clergyman'.

Charles Darwin,
who graduated in 1831 from Cambridge with a BA - in natural history and geology!

Charles Darwin,
who, as resident naturalist, sailed to the Galapagos Islands on the HMS Beagle, where he encountered evidence

> "of great diversity between animals of the distant past and those of the present." *(www.progressivetheology.org)*

It was following this trip and as a result of him being unable to reconcile his fundamentalist beliefs with his speculations about the origin of species, that

> "...in the months following his return... his new scientific theory was born and his faith in religion was dead."
> *(Birch 2008:116)*

Away from home for five years, Darwin returned home in 1836 with new purpose. He no longer considered going into the church - even a country parish -
    and was recognised as a man of scientific authority,
    and approved of by his father.

Charles Darwin,
who gave us his most famous major work
called *'On The Origin of Species'*, a treatise

> "providing extensive evidence for the evolution of organisms and proposing natural selection as the key process determining its course" *(Ayala 2007: 61)*

which he published nearly 160 years ago - on 24 November 1859.

Published... yes. But it would appear just a little reluctantly.
About the decision to publish his thoughts it has been suggested
    that he was pulled in two directions.

> "His theory of evolution had a reforming, anti-establishment appeal. It is said that he thought like a Unitarian but felt for the Cambridge clerics who had helped to make his career and reputation. Above all else, he knew his theory de-throned a Creator God, challenged the most cherished beliefs of the Christian church and diminished the special status of humankind. Another source of conflict was his beloved wife Emma's Christian belief in salvation and fear that his views would prevent their union in an afterlife." *(Kirk 2009)*

The book was immediately recognised as a naturalistic explanation of one of the deep questions, one that had hitherto been in the province of religion:
    'Where did we come from?'

Darwin suggested that the world or universe was:
- (i) unfinished and continuing;
- (ii) involved chance events and struggle, and
- (iii) natural selection took the place of

"design according to a preordained [divine] blueprint." *(Birch 1965:29)*

The whole universe is alive and changing, continually co-creating new possibilities of life.
 Change is!

Or as evolutionary theist, Prof. Howard van Till, a member of '3C Community' in USA, said to his then pastor about genetic variation and natural selection:

> "Spontaneous genetic variation is the way that Earth's ecosystem explores new possibilities for life forms. No exploration = nothing new to look forward to. Thank 'God' for genetic exploration.

> "Natural selection = go with whatever happens to work best at this time and place. That implies that the future will be interesting but admits that the details are yet to be worked out. This approach preserves the possibility of surprise. Thank 'God' for surprise." *(Aussie Heretic blog site, 2006)*

Or put even another way, change is the core of cosmic evolution, biological evolution, cultural/symbolic evolution. *(Peters 2002, Kaufman 2004)*

ooOoo

In every age, the worlds of theology and religion interact with the cultural and scientific world views of that day.
Such interaction between the two, in the words of feminist Catholic theologian Elizabeth Johnson,

"is essential to make religious faith both credible and relevant within a particular generation's view of the world and how it works." *(Johnson 2007:286)*

But Johnson goes on:

"In sum, theological reflection today should endeavor to speak about God's relation not to an ancient nor medieval nor Newtonian world, but to the dynamic, emergent, self-organizing universe that contemporary natural and biological sciences describe." *(Johnson 2007:287)*

Scientists tell us the 'Great Story', as we understand it today, begins with the ultimate mystery of the (misnamed) Big Bang, some 14 billion years ago.
Life on Earth originated some 4.5+ billion years ago.

Homo habilis (our ancestors) begin using tools 2.5 million years ago. Symbolic language emerges between 50,000 and 500,000 years ago.
Classical religions emerge around 3,000 - 4,000 years ago.
I – the trillions of cells that make up my body – emerged nearly 74 years ago!

Billions of years of cosmic evolution have produced us.
The ancestral stars are a part of our genealogy.

Everything in the universe is related.

"Can you feel that umbilical cord to the Cosmos?" suggests

another.

"Can you feel the strands of connectedness – the interdependent web – of all existence, even with all human beings?" *(DeWolf 2008)*

The traditional model of life with the god God as king and ruler, described as omnipotent, sustaining the world's development through pre-programmed attributes, and intervening miraculously from the outside when and wherever, is

"less and less seriously imaginable." *(Johnson 2007:291)*

On the other hand, Alfred North Whitehead, the Anglo-American process philosopher and mathematician,
describes life as an adventure. He felt that:

> "novelty and surprise made life interesting. The open-endedness of life provides opportunities for the exercise of creative freedom, which gives life meaning."
> *(Christ 2003:171).*

I agree. And this is why on this day for the past twelve years, we have celebrated Evolution Sunday/Weekend.

And this is why I have often thought of the god G-o-d:
- as the creative process or 'creativity', rather than a being who creates, and
- as I continue to search for non-personal metaphors for G-o-d or the sacred

rather than personal, anthropological ones.

ooOoo

Contemporary progressive theology reminds us time and time again, G-o-d or the sacred does not reside in some other place called 'heaven'.

Nor is heaven our goal. The world is our true home.

Indeed, our only home.

"This life is meant to be enjoyed," writes Carol Christ.
> "To enjoy life is to cherish the beauty of each living thing, to be interested in diversity and difference in the web of life…" *(Christ 2003:116)*

May the story of the one who renders impotent the power of dirt to keep the 'unclean' outside the human community…

And the story of the ones who discovered the whole universe is alive and changing, continually, and
> that novelty and surprise makes life interesting…
>> always awaken within us new possibilities for the now.

Notes

Ayala, F. J. *"The Evolution of Life: An Overview"* in M. K. Cunningham. (ed.) **God and Evolution. A Reader.** Oxon. Routledge, 2007.
Birch, L. C. **Science and Soul.** Sydney. The University of NSW Press, 2008.
– – – – -, **Nature and God.** London. SCM Press, 1965.
Christ, C. P. **She Who Changes. Re-imagining the Divine in the World.** New York. PalgraveMacmillan, 2003.
DeWolf, M. L. *"What do we Mean – 'Thank God for Evolution'?"* A Sermon. Nature Coast Unitarian Universalists Church. *The Clergy Letter Project* web site, 2008.
Johnson, E. A. *"Does God Play Dice? Divine Providence and Chance"* in M. K. Cunningham. (ed) **God and Evolution. A Reader.** Oxon. Routledge, 2007.
Kaufman, G. D. **In the Beginning... Creativity.** Minneapolis. Fortress Press, 2004.
Kirk, M. (ed.). *"Worship Resource Material from the The General Assembly of Unitarian and Free Christian Churches, London, recognising the 200th anniversary of the birth of Charles Darwin."* 2009.
Ian Lawton. 'Aussie heretic blog site'.
Patterson, S. J. *"Dirt, Shame, and Sin"* in R. W Hoover. (ed.) **Profiles of Jesus.** Santa Rosa. Polebridge Press, 2002.
Peters, K. E. **Dancing with the Sacred. Evolution, Ecology, and God.** Harrisburg. Trinity International, 2002.
Wilson, L. (ed.) **Charles Darwin at Down House.** Bristol, UK. English Heritage, 1998.

SHAPING THE MARROW OF EVERY STONE

Look with me
Into the heart of a stone

Which One? There are so many!
Whatever one calls you into seeing

The stone that owns you
That sits in your collection of possibilities

Hold it secure in thumb and two fingers
Rotating its presence in growing wonder
Observing its well-owned idiosyncrasies
Fissures --- texture --- lustre

Admire its many possibilities of becoming
Formed in the crucible of planetary fire
Formed in an archaic seabed
Lifted in the techtonic-dance of deep-time

Pressured into the joy of new awakenings
In the tight grip of the protective Mother

And then what of those discarded gems
Those forgotten pieces in the debris
Of this Anthropocean Geology?
So many bits!!!

Now look closer
With imagining-eyes
And the late knowing of things

Look pass the intensity
Of atoms in their intense motion
Held together in unfailing attraction

Discover here the lucidity of star-dust
And own in your core-being
The likeness of like

Fleeting as yours and mine maybe

John Cranmer
February 2016

Theme focus: Desert/Wilderness

10. MATE, THE DESERT IS G-O-D'S OWN COUNTRY...

> "When swimming in turbulent waters,
> wisdom lies in knowing when to relax and when to struggle."
> *(Sam Keen)*

This week religious season called Lent commenced.
    It began on the earthy day designated as Ash Wednesday.

Because on that day, as tradition would have it,
the church remembers we are people of the earth
    and to symbolise that,
    a mark with ash is placed on our foreheads…

> "Ash Wednesday invites us to come back to earth.
> To wonder at the gift of life,
>   my life
>   our life
> with the earth, the shared body of our existence.
>
> "These ashes were once trees and shrubs,
> and places where life was lived to its fullest.
>
> "Once they were full of life.
> Now they are black and grey.
>   Dry.
>   Lifeless.

> "But mixed with the waters of our baptism
> make good fertiliser:
> it will help the seeds of the gospel take deeper root in us
> > and bring forth the fruits,
> > > the harvest of justice, peace, and generosity.
>
> "These are ashes worth wearing.
> May we accept this gift. And be blessed.
> > And be assured we will be different at the end of this season.
>
> "For from the burnt ashes will spring the green shoot of life
> and the purple flower of attentiveness to God."
> > *(Hunt, Liturgy for Ash Wednesday)*

Lent is also associated with the story of Jesus/Yeshu'a in the desert or wilderness.
Australian author and poet Bruce Prewer plays with this image of desert and tellingly suggests:

> "The dire danger to the adventurer
> is not demoralising gibber plains
> nor ridge after ridge of sand,
> but the distracting lure
> of the shimmering
> mirage.

'The shimmering mirage', I know it well,
having been brought up in the dry Wimmera area of Victoria
> and journeyed many times into the Little Desert!

But Prewer takes this image even further:

> "To distinguish reality from the illusion
> and to keep one's bearings and course
> in spite of the mind's treachery -
> this is the ultimate test
> for the pilgrims
> and prophets.

Then he brings it home to the reality of city people, especially those who never venture into the outback or desert areas:

"City prophets have a variation on this word:
Deserts take victims swiftly, savagely,
but urban mirages work slowly,
day by day diverting prey
and destroying souls
still smiling." *(Prewer 1996)*

ooOoo

What do people mean when they talk of deserts?
Indeed, what is a desert?

Limiting my comments to Australia…
Australia has ten named deserts, the largest being the Great Victoria Desert
    which crosses the border into both Western Australia and South Australia.
        It is over 800 kilometres wide
        and covers an area of 348,750 square kilometres.

In total, the ten deserts cover 1,371,000 square kilometres
or 18% of the Australian mainland.
    However, approximately 35% of the Australian continent receives so little rain it is effectively desert.
        Result? Australia has been called the driest continent on earth.
The perception of what is a desert or wilderness area varies greatly, depending on the different exposures people have
to nature and the 'great outdoors'.

For instance, some historians claim that for the first white settlers
in New South Wales (Australia)
the landscape seemed barren, uninhabited,
> desolate - even hostile -
> because it lacked the plants and animals of Europe.

However, according to Australian historian Grace Karskens,
the Sydney environment, for instance, was described as both
> 'very romantic, beautifully formed by nature'
> as well as 'the worst country in the world'.

Why such discrepancy?
Conditions for the convicts and early settlers were harsh.
> For example, the drive to clear the dense bushland of the ever-creeping vegetation, and establish public farms, was to establish the initial food supply for the prison colony.
>> But such conditions were also presented and remembered as places of torment and brutality.

Karskens notes:

> "There were tales of convicts buried alive, convicts eating grass, convicts summarily hanged, convicts the helpless victims of both sadistic overseers and officers, who also lusted after their wives." *(Karskens 2009:94)*

Farming was primitive and the farmers lived in poverty.

But, there was also a 'rage for curiosity' back home in Europe
A curiosity that was filled by the later free-settlers - authors and artists of various skills -
> almost as soon as they disembarked in Sydney.

Inspired to capture the beauty of what they saw, they were bursting to tell their family and friends about their experiences.

"Everyone who could write, or dictate a letter, took the trouble to describe the plants, animals and native inhabitants of the new land [using the language of wonder, beauty and emotion rather than science] for their friends and relatives back home, or in the manuscripts they were preparing for their publishers. The European foundations of Australia were marked by a great outpouring of art and writing by the 'eager curiosity' of these self-conscious discoverers."
(Karskens 2009:256)

ooOoo

Authors, poets, and artists often reminded us that
most people see deserts as places lacking the life forms
    that are significant to them.

To a person living on the coast, the desert is often dry and arid and dusty. A place without life.
    But for desert dwellers in Australia's 'outback'
    it has a compelling fascination, as a place vibrant with life.

The spinifex are blue grey with amber glints.
They look soft but they are prickly and hard.
    They survive tenaciously
    because no grazing animal can eat them out
    or destroy their roots.

It may look as if nothing can live in the desert,
but underneath the spinifex,
    the desert creatures leave their tracks in the red sand.

No life stirs all day, but come night...
    lizards, mice, and the rare animals of the desert
    live their delicate but vastly tough lives in this harsh habitat.
The desert is the place where one does not expect to find life.
Yet life is present.

If we only see the desert as a place of harsh, relentlessness...
where people face despair and animals die of thirst,
    the desert will always be an alien danger.

ooOoo

Back to our gospel 'desert' story...
"Still wet from his baptism in the Jordan..."
    as professor of preaching Fred Craddock puts it so eloquently,
    Jesus goes out into the wilderness, into the desert.

And in the desert, our storyteller Matthew *(Matthew 4:1-11)* says Jesus encountered Satan.
'Satan' is the translation of a Hebrew word which means: "adversary, wicked opponent".
    Someone who opposes, accuses, slanders - is Satan.
    A contemporary interpretation of the meaning of this word is 'hinderer'.

The major focus of Matthew's story, it seems to me,
is on Jesus having certain powers which Matthew assumes he has,
    and on saying 'no' to certain models of action.
Most are familiar with those options.

One option offered by 'the hinderer'
is to gain followers through stunts or miracles.
    A common option then and now.

Another is to take the military option: achieve dominion by force.
    Those of the Religious and Political Right
        believe that is the option in Iraq or North Korea or Syria.

While yet another could be to join the revolutionary movements of the day.

Australian biblical scholar William Loader reminds us:

> "Such traditions and expectations colour the gospel accounts of Jesus' ministry. We can be sure that many would have listened to the fantasy of Jesus' great trial with such things in mind."
> *(Loader Web site, 2001)*

All these options, storyteller Matthew takes from a mass of stories circulating in and around his community about this itinerant peasant sage.
    Yet with a sense of real concern, he offers them
        as a teaching opportunity to his young congregation.

Empowering them to discerning where G-o-d is in the world.

And because we know the end of this story,
we know Jesus survives the experience of being in the desert,
    and returns to move throughout Galilee.

ooOoo

But what's this got to do with Lent?
In response, let me offer a suggestion and a story.

Lent is a very real time where many can once again, in an intentional way, seek out the presentness of the sacred
    lurking in the most unlikely of places,
        waiting to be uncovered, found, and embraced.

And the story... A Zen teacher said to his students:

  'If you raise a speck of dust, the nation flourishes,
  but the elders furrow their brows.

    'If you don't raise a speck of dust, the nation perishes,
    but the elders relax their brows.'
A speck of dust - what is that?

What kind of power lies in a speck of dust?

Well… if we listen to cosmologists they say
we are made from dust – (electron, quarks, gluons, higgs, graviton, etc.) – stardust.
> We are all connected – biologically and spiritually – with planet Earth and with all its 'other than human' beings.

> "…organically connected to the trees, to the water splashing against the shoreline, to the squirrels running around collecting nuts, and to the birds who sang me into each new day. I knew myself to be biologically and geologically kin, fashioned from the same supernova stardust." *(Sanguin 2007:26)*

While (now late) American Priest Harry Cook suggested:

> "One thing is certain in life, besides death and taxes. It is dust. Tons of it fall on Earth every day. A goodly portion of it winds up on my desk. And when I think on it, I realize that some of that substance is composed of what's left of biological life, including that of other human beings." *(Cook 2017)*

If we talk to anyone with dust in her or his computer,
> or digital sound system,
> or on a contact lens,
> you will certainly get another kind of answer!

But I suggest our Zen teacher had a different or third answer in mind. To raise a speck of dust is to
> stir up goodness,
> struggle for justice,
> speak up for those who stutter or do not speak the languages of power,
> band together to stand resolutely and non violently before evil
>> and refuse to be absorbed into it
>> or intimidated by it.

For some people, Lent is a time of sorry self-deprecation.
But I am not helped by that.

Instead, I reckon Lent can be a time when,
in positive and intentional ways,
> our actions can enable others to flourish.

When our selfless actions seep into the world
'like the scent of perfume distilled in the air'...
> encouraging and giving fresh heart to those around us,
> and strengthening the bonds of community.

So the real story behind the so-called 'temptation' stories about this peasant Jewish sage without family, friends, property, or job, is
> he really does have something to offer us.

For, at the core, Jesus was a person of extraordinary religious insight. He was utterly convinced of the connectedness
> between human loving and living in G-o-d.

He was passionate about setting people free
> from ideas and images about G-o-d that enslaved them.

And he invited people to believe that through their
> everyday acts of human kindness
> they are intimately connected with each other, the world,
> and the sacred.

ooOoo

The desert is a place where one does not expect to find life.
A god-forsaken place.

But following his desert experience, maybe Jesus was able to claim:
'mate, this is g-o-d's own country!'

May that be our experience during the Lenten season.
And may we remember in our dry seasons that we, too,
are desert flowers.

Notes

Cook, H. T. *"Dust to Dust"*. **Harry T. Cook Essay.** (29 September 2017) <revharrytcook@aol.com>
Karskens, G. **The Colony. A History of Early Sydney.** Crows Nest. Allen & Unwin, 2009.
Keen, S. **Apology for Wonder.** New York. Harper & Row, 1969.
Prewer, B. D. **More Australian Psalms.** Adelaide. OpenBook Publishers, 1996.
Sanguin, B. **Darwin, Divinity, and the Dance of the Cosmos. An Ecological Christianity.** Kelowna. CopperHouse, 2007.

REWILDING SUBURBIA

Come with me
Together may we discover
A recovering edge of wildness
Here in this overgrowing
Suburban plot
Finding a new way
Through the unexpected gifts
Of time and neglect
Astonishing Life resurging
From out this wiped-clean
Piece of alienated land
Severed from
Its geological-forming
Minutely surveyed
Earth memory sanitised
Almost out of existence
Under the scouring
Of 'dozer-blades
And the imposed-infertility
Of bitumen and poured-concrete

But now see this place
Quietly overwhelmed
With life returning
In the cracks of possibility
Offering
Some kind of remembering
Remaking and reviving

John Cranmer
December 2016

Theme focus: Advent/Ordinary

11. ADVENT: THE SACRED IN THE ORDINARY AND SYMBOLIC...

> "For too long we have attempted to understand reality
> solely through reason and have forgotten the importance of
> symbolic narrative, metaphor, and the sacred story."
> *(John Westerhoff)*

Today we continue our journey into the season of Advent.
The season that heralds the start of a new church year.

In spite of the northern hemisphere flavour of it all,
with its ancient cosmology and seasonal irrelevance,
> we have started on a journey of
> > waiting, preparing, seeing, understanding.

However, this new church year did not start with a celebration
of something that had happened.
> Such as stories of a birth or a resurrection.

Instead, it started with a strange ordinariness - even emptiness.

Last week also showed how the designers of the Lectionary
delved way into the collection of stories
> by the storyteller we call Mark.

And there they found, and grabbed, a certain kind of story.
A story often regarded by many interpreters
as an apocalyptic warning
> about the end times.

And they dropped this so-called end time story
right at the beginning of the season and the year.
> Stay awake! Keep alert!

Why?
Otherwise we may miss what actually is.
Otherwise we may miss the signs of the presentness
> of an incognito G-o-d/the sacred in the midst of ordinary events.

Or if we want to follow Mark's line of thought:
otherwise you will miss the importance of the ending of my story,
> so get the beginning clues locked into your brain!

And here comes a couple of the storyteller's *(Mark 1:1-8)* early clues:
> a human messiah, and
> a bloke called John.

ooOoo

First, and not getting too technical, the hope for a Jewish human messiah was given new impetus around the time of Yeshu'a/Jesus' birth.
> Not because of his birth, but because
> of the death of one ruthless ruler, Herod the Great.

From what we can figure out, the anonymous storyteller we call Mark, writing some forty years at least after Jesus, saw that
> Jesus was indeed 'messiah', even a **political** messiah,
> but not a nationalistic zealot messiah.

Mark's vision of 'messiah' was about creating a commonwealth of people who were seeking "harmony with themselves, with the whole human species, and with the total social and natural environment." *(Cairns 2004:6)*

Even the storyteller's use of the word 'gospel' or 'good news'
has about it the older Roman political sense of 'victory in battle',
    although later on it also becomes influenced
    by Greek sensibilities and tends to refer
    to life stories of heroic figures.

So combining 'messiah' and 'good news' perhaps we can say:

"Mark sees the Jesus story as laying the foundations for a new humanitarian attitude of people toward people, and of society towards its members." *(Cairns 2004:7)*

    Second, from all we do (which sometimes is not much), and
    do not know the bloke called John the baptiser,
    or 'dipper', simply appears.

From all we do and do not know, tradition has it
John spent some fourteen years in the desert wilderness.
    And when he emerged, he came as a somewhat wild,
    austere man, dressed in animal skins,
    and eating Kosher locusts,
        which he washed down with gulps of wild honey.

For many people, including our storyteller Mark and a later one we call Luke, John was a prophet.
Indeed, not just any ordinary prophet,
    but the 'reincarnation' of the prophet Elijah.

John is primarily remembered for his 'baptisms', *(Tatum 1994)*
and for his preaching - 'repentance' and 'forgiveness of sins'.
    But not 'repentance' and 'forgiveness' as modern day
    fundamentalists claim.

New Zealander Ian Cairns is helpful here, I reckon. He writes:

> "proclaiming a baptism of repentance for the forgiveness of sins means inviting the hearers-readers to make tangible if symbolic expression of their willingness to embrace a new way of looking at things, and commit themselves to a new vision of 'commonwealth'..." *(Cairns 2004:9)*

John, who probably was in his mid to late 20s, spent his youth and early adult years as a hermit in the desert wilderness.
    Why? Well, we also need to hear and understand
        just how important the desert wilderness was
            in Israel's foundational stories.

Some suggestions include:
- The desert wilderness was the place, in the time of Moses, where the Israelites believed they had met God.
    So it was the place where they learned about
    their role as a holy people.

- The desert wilderness was a place of testing.
A place of preparation. A place of vulnerability.
    Where a person was stripped of all pretensions
    and found out what he or she was really like.

- The desert wilderness was a place of appalling danger and deprivation.

So storyteller Mark links John to the past. An important past.
But he is also seen to be a present-day forerunner of the future.

In his book ***Liberating the Gospels***, Bishop John Shelby Spong writes:

"John was thus created or, perhaps more accurately, shaped to be the Elijah type messenger and forerunner. John became the life that the Christians believed was foretold [in the Hebrew scriptures]." *(Spong 1996:195)*

But... I reckon our storyteller Mark
has something else in mind as well.
Something more than John just being a prophet.
    And that something more is about giving 'honour'.

Everything Mark says about John seems to bolster his status as a prophet. And, therefore, his honour. So when Mark has John say:
    'Someone is following me, someone
    who is more powerful than I am...'
I reckon we can also hear that as a prod from storyteller Mark:
    'This someone who is more powerful, more worthy,
    deserves our honour more than John does.'

In the hands of Mark, storyteller, John the dipper
is both a prophet in his own right, and one who becomes
    the precursor to Jesus, another more honourable prophet.

On the linkage between the two, between John and Jesus,
perhaps Ian Cairns'comment can be again helpful:

"Just as John's baptism symbolised the willingness to commit oneself to the vision of 'commonwealth', so Jesus by his teaching and example, and by the inspiring impact of his personality, will make available the dynamic for the commitment... For Mark and his community, the ministry of Jesus makes this enduring dynamic accessible is a new way." *(Cairns 2004:10)*

ooOoo

So what might this say about Advent today?
Look for the clues of this incognito, community-building god G-o-d all around you.
>Stay awake! Be alert!

Advent is a time to be surprised by the ordinary
and empowered by the symbolic as we re-imagine the world.

Taking a clue from the words of the peasant Galilean sage
as suggested by professor of religious studies, Charles Hedrick:

> "His actual words dealt more with lower class village life in the early Roman Empire than it did with a philosophical probing of the Judea state religion, or in setting out a specific code of conduct for daily life – rather, he dealt generally in sweeping unrealistic challenges to daily life rather than in positing narrow legal rules to be followed as a code of conduct, and he leaves vague the practical decision as to how his ideas should be incorporated into daily life."
> *(Hedrick 2014:84)*

And Advent is a time to discover the ordinary given moments in our daily events:
- in the click-clack of two branches knocking together in the wind...
- in the realisation that rain is not a singular thing
  but made up of billions of individual drops of water,
  each with its own destination and timing...
- in the mating song of a blackbird high in eucalyptus tree...
- in the flares of a friend's passion to shape justice
  with a new vision of 'commonwealth'...

These are Advent moments. These are sacred moments.
Sensing the presentness of the sacred in the ordinary
and the symbolic
>as we live out our daily lives.

May we have the wisdom to see and honour, understand and celebrate, this pre-Christmas season called Advent!

Notes

Cairns, I. J. **Mark of a Non-Realist. A Contemporary Reading of the Second Gospel.** Masterton. Fraser Books, 2004.
Hedrick, C. W. **The Wisdom of Jesus. Between the Sages of Israel and the Apostles of the Church.** Eugene. Cascade Books, 2014.
Spong, J. S. **Liberating the Gospels. Reading the Bible with Jewish Eyes.** New York. HarperCollins, 1996.
Tatum, W. B. *"John the Baptist and Jesus".* A Report of the Jesus Seminar. 1994. In private circulation.
Westerhoff, J. H. *"Contemporary Spirituality: Revelation, Myth and Ritual"* in G. Durka & J. Smith. (eds). **Aesthetic Dimensions of Religious Education.** New York. Paulist Press, 1979.

BLACKBIRDS AT FIRST LIGHT

To be awake
To the morning
With the joy
Of Blackbirds
Offering each day
As new creation

We who together
Have found our place
In a strange land
In which
To bring a melody
Not known before

Here is melody
That forgets the past
Yet remembering
That vital awareness
That makes
All things NEW

And the Blackbird
Has moved on
Into the coming light
And together
We seize the day
Potent and Becoming

John Cranmer
November 2015

Theme focus: Apocalyptic/End Times

12. WHEN RELIGIOUS PEOPLE CAN BE DOWN-RIGHT SILLY!

"Religious practices, ideas and beliefs are meant to
aid human emancipation.
They are not cages, designed to contain or repress human beings.
They are for making us free."
(Don Cupitt)

There are many ways religious people can look silly.
A certain Australian Catholic cardinal has made a name for himself as a denier of radical climate change.
Which makes him look even sillier.

An Anglican bishop's comments were much harsher than mine, saying the cardinal's statements on climate change were
"almost unbelievable."

So too the parliamentary courtyard goings-on
of the fundamentalist group, 'Catch the Fire Ministries'.

Both remind me of the story about a bloke who was always having bad luck. Once he found a magic lamp, rubbed it, and
a genie appeared and gave him the midas touch.

For the rest of his life, everything he touched
turned into a muffler! *(Bausch 1998:390)*

Our biblical story this morning from a
pseudo-Pauline letter *(2 Thessalonians)*, is also one such silly time.
    So let me unpack some of this
        by sharing some contextual stuff first.

                      ooOoo

I am not aware of any reputable biblical scholar who agrees
that this so-called Pauline letter, was written by Paul.
        The evidence points to someone using Paul's name to claim
        authority, while writing sometime after Paul.

John Dominic Crossan, probably one of the leading biblical scholars
of our time, is clear in his statement.
        There are authentic Paul letters and
        there are pseudo Paul letters.

The authentic letters can be named:
        Romans, 1 and 2 Corinthians, Galatians,
        Philippians, 1 Thessalonians, Philemon.

The inauthentic or post Pauline letters, attributed to Paul
but not written by Paul, include:
        Ephesians, Colossians, 2 Thessalonians,
        1 and 2 Timothy, Titus.

Some people I know have their favourite Paul bits.
But do your favourite bits of Paul belong in the
        authentic Paul basket or in the pseudo Paul basket?
                It can make a lot of difference, you know.

Not only are there pseudo Paul letters, but some
of those letters are anti-Paul letters, as evidenced by much of the
        content of Ephesians and Timothy, so relied on by
        fundamentalists and neo-orthodox these days
        for their 'anti' causes!

Why the anti Paul letters?
Well, Crossan suggests, they are an

> "attempt to sanitize a social subversive, to domesticate a dissident apostle, and to make Christianity and Rome safe for one another."
> *(Crossan & Reed 2004:106)*

Which kind of brings us back to today's biblical story.
(2 Thessalonians 2:16 to 3:5)

Some of the author's hearers are frightened.
They seem convinced that the so-called 'second coming of Jesus' is about to happen.
> So they have got themselves all into a lather.
> And their goings-on have divided their small community.

The author tries to counter this 'apocalyptic scenario', but to no avail. Instead the comments seem to pour oil onto troubled fires.

Palpable fear grips the Thessalonians.
Such as some politicians hope will happen
during an election campaign.
> For fear speaks louder than either history or reasoned debate!

Being progressives, we can dismiss all this 'apocalyptic', 'end-of-the-world', 'second-coming-of-Jesus' stuff as fanciful rubbish.
> And most of it is. Or if you prefer Bishop Jack Spong's evaluation:
>> "gobbledygook and complete non-sense."
>> *(Spong NewsLetter, 31.10.07)*

Especially the modern writings of Tim LeHaye and the "transcendental snake oil" *(Crossan 2007:198)*
called the Left Behind series.
> As well as the rantings of many American TV evangelists, and their Australian imitators.

So it is important to try and go under the apocalyptic veneer in order to get in touch with the real underlying issue.

And that real issue is, I suggest:
> not about the end of the world or the second coming of Jesus,
> but about the end of evil and injustice and violence... in this world.

On the former, Crossan is again helpful:

> "The Second Coming of Christ is not an event that we should expect to happen *soon*. The Second Coming of Christ is not an event that we should expect to happen *violently*. The Second Coming of Christ is not an event that we should expect to happen *literally*. The Second Coming of Christ is what will happen when we Christians finally accept that the First Coming was the Only Coming and start to cooperate with divine presence." *(Crossan 2007:230-231)*

On the latter, a professor of religion and philosophy, Russell Pregeant, says we need to get in touch with:

> "the hope for peace and justice that has led many in our own time, under the influence of liberation theology, to speak of apocalyptic writings as 'the literature of the oppressed'." *(Pregeant, P&F web site, 2007)*

And Pregeant goes on to say:

> "[this is] a reminder that God is certainly not satisfied with the unjust structure of the present world... [But] we need neither the outrageous fantasies of the so-called 'rapture' nor the grotesque images of millions of souls condemned to eternal torture while the blessed shine like the sun, to insure that human life has eternal significance." *(Pregeant, P&F web site, 2007)*

ooOoo

What are we left with?
Apocalyptic talk, in our own times, that wants to claim
> a basis in divine destruction, is unhelpful.

Apocalyptic talk, in our own times, that wants to claim
a basis in human transformation, is helpful.
> It is that simple.

But for us to get beyond this helpful/unhelpful dichotomy,
something more is required of us. And that is to:
> (i) read and study the biblical stories seriously, not literally, and
> (ii) know that we, even if only in a small way, are called upon to participate in the transformation of the world.

If we are only against something, we are doomed to negativity.
So too if our actions are only attempts
at domesticating dissident voices,
> making religion and politics safe for one another.

Something which Parliament House-going fundamentalist Christians, and 'want-to-be-re-elected' politicians of any party,
> need to remember!

Notes

Bausch, W. J. **A World of Stories for Preachers and Teachers.** Mystic. Twenty-Third Publications, 1998.
Crossan, J. D. **God and Empire. Jesus Against Rome, Then and Now.** New York. HarperCollins, 2007.
Crossan, J. D. & J. L. Reed. **In Search of Paul. How Jesus's Apostle Opposed Rome's Empire with God's Kingdom.** New York. HarperSanFrancisco, 2004.
Cupitt, D. **Rethinking Religion.** Wellington. St. Andrew's Trust, 1992.

Theme focus: Ocean

13. THE EARTH THAT WE KNEW, IS GONE. LONG LIVE EAARTH!

"All human traditions are dimensions of each other. If, as Christians, we assert the Christian dimension of the entire world, we must not refuse to be a dimension
of the Hindu world, of the Buddhist world, of the Islamic world. Upon this intercommunion on a planetary scale depends the future development of the human community.
This is the creative task of our times, to foster the global meeting of the nations and of the world's spiritual traditions."
(Thomas Berry)

We are living in a scientific, pluralistic age.
And unless you have been living under a cabbage leaf,
    then you will also be aware of the
    current universal debates about how

        "our modern life-style is harming other creatures, diminishing the functioning of ecosystems, and altering our global climate patterns." *(Peters 2002:viii)*

Planet Earth is in peril. All creation is suffering.
As you can imagine or already know,
several folk have put their concerns
    in books,
    during workshops,
    at political rallies and conferences; and
    via the media.

The focus for today's sermon/address - Ocean - comes out of
the Lectionary season... The Season of Creation.

This particular year the themes for the month are Ocean,
Fauna, Storm, and Cosmos.
> So I would like to think it is important stuff
> we are again saying and doing this morning.

ooOoo

Life seems to have started under water.
Scientists claim that life within the ocean evolved some
> three billion years prior to life on land.

The molecular building blocks for Earth life
> are thought to have accumulated in the waters of Earth
> > from the time it formed – about 4.5+ billion years ago,
> > creating what scientists call the 'primal soup'.

And as the story goes: it's all in the chemistry!

I am informed that approximately 71% of the earth's surface
is covered by ocean – a continuous body of water that is
> customarily divided into several principal oceans
> and smaller seas.

More than half of this area is over 3,000 metres deep.
And the collective volume is approximately
1.3 billion cubic kilometres.

And they estimate that 230,000 marine life-forms of all types
are currently known, but the total could be
> up to 10 times that number.

Added to these facts...
- Oceanic life forms began three (3) billion years ago.
In comparison, land-based creatures appeared only 400 million years ago.
- A mouthful of water from the ocean contains millions of bacteria and billions of viruses.

There are five main Earth's oceans:
    The Pacific Ocean is the largest of the oceans, followed by
    the Atlantic Ocean, the Indian Ocean, the Arctic Ocean,
    and the Southern Ocean.

We also know that the ocean has a significant effect on the biosphere. Oceanic evaporation as a phase of the water cycle
    is the source of most rainfall and ocean temperatures
    determine both climate and wind patterns
    that affect life on land.

But... the oceans, the sea, that 71% of the earth's surface we usually don't consider much outside our summer vacations,
    is changing due to global warming.
And in Australia that 'change' is most noticeable
    when inland drought hits!

To raise awareness on the state of the world's oceans
World Oceans Day is celebrated in June.
    A recent theme was: 'Our Oceans, Our Future',
    while the conservation action focus was on
        encouraging solutions to plastic pollution
        and preventing marine litter, for a healthier ocean and a better future.

ooOoo

As I was preparing the original draft of this Address,
I was reading Bill McKibben's book, **Ea*r*th: Making a Life on a Tough New Planet.**
It certainly made an impression on me!

The media were telling me the BP oil slick in the Gulf of Mexico was continuing to grow, and all attempts to stem its flow
were proving to be in vain.

Indeed, in a radio interview on *ABC Radio National* Breakfast, McKibben said we will really sense God's humour
when the hurricane season strikes…
they will go further inland and live longer, due to the sun's rays being absorbed by the dark surface of the oil, warming the air, dropping even more record rain.

Bill McKibben is an author and founder of the environmental organisations *Step It Up* and *350.org*
and was one of the first to warn
of the dangers of global warming.

I invite you to read a selection of just some of Bill McKibben's comments on oceans and climate warming:

"The oceans… are distinctly more acid and their level is rising; they are also warmer, which means the greatest storms of our planet, hurricanes and cyclones, have become more powerful". *(McKibben 2010:45)*

How come?
Because of our emissions and our burning of cheap fossil fuel, a process

"that Britain's Royal Society described as 'essentially irreversible'." *(McKibben 2010:10)*

To make his point further, McKibben says:

> "One barrel of oil yields as much energy as 25,000 hours of human manual labor – more than a decade of human labor per barrel. The average American uses 25 barrels each year, which is like finding 300 years of free labor annually. And that's just the oil; there's coal and gas, too." *(McKibben 2010:27)*

Economics and growth have become the watchwords for modernity!

At the same time, research is showing the earth's ice caps and glaciers are melting with "disconcerting and unexpected speed." *(McKibben 2010:45)*
>   We have already raised the temperature nearly a degree Celsius.

McKibben continues:

> "…the ocean is more acid than anytime in the last eight hundred thousand years, and at current rates by 2050 it will be more corrosive than anytime in the past 20 million years." *(McKibben 2010:10)*

And again:

> "On the last day of 2008, the Economist reported that temperatures on the Antarctic Peninsula were rising faster than anywhere else on earth, and that the West Antarctic was losing ice 75 percent faster than just a decade before… Name a major feature of the earth's surface and you'll find massive change." *McKibben 2010:5)*

The changes could hardly be more fundamental!

> "The earth that we knew – the only earth that we ever knew – is gone." *(McKibben 2010:27)*

ooOoo

If you are beginning to hear 'doomsday' and 'apocalypse'
then I guess I can't blame you.
    I had the same feelings as I read McKibben's book.

We can be numbed by all the figures and percentages.
We can say the scientists are probably overstating our woes.
    The anticipated future can be paralysed by our fears.

Indeed, it's hard to brace ourselves

> "for the jump to a new world when we still, kind of, live in the old one... We're so used to growth that we can't imagine alternatives; at best we embrace the squishy sustainable, with its implied claim that we can keep on as before."
> *(McKibben 2010:102)*

Well, McKibben is not all negative and alarmist.
He does offer some suggestions – some words – for change.
    And those five words are: Durable, Sturdy, Stable,
    Hardy, Robust.

And for of us that all means reshaping our society:
- from big to smaller,
- from growth to maintenance,
- from expansion to scale down,
- from global to neighbourhood.

But you'll have to read his book!

ooOoo

Human beings, especially in the so-called 'West', have historically been reluctant to consider themselves as part of the web of nature.
    Indeed a web within a web.

Likewise, Australia does not have a good record when it comes to climate change. Governments since the early 1990s have all adopted a strategy
>of more-or-less do little to nothing at home
>and work hard to prevent others from taking major action.

So there has been an encouragement of community
and media apathy.

Not to mention the often cosy relationships between the fossil-fuel lobbyists, called the 'greenhouse mafia' – which consists of the executive directors of a handful
>of industry associations in the coal, oil, cement, aluminium, mining and electricity industries – and many politicians,
>>all exposed by a 2006 ABC Four Corners TV program, and Clive Hamilton's book, **Scorcher: The Dirty Politics of Climate Change.**

If our biblical tradition suggests anything, human beings are part of nature. The problems comes when Christians – usually fundamentalists –
>claim that the mythical stories of Genesis 1 and 2,
>are more 'true' or more 'factual' than science and evolution.

So in many quarters there is a raging attack on 'progressive' religion:
> • from fundamentalists who don't believe one can accept evolution and be religious; and
> • from the 'new atheists' who caricature all people of religion as fundamentalists. *(Michael Zimmerman.* **The Clergy Letter Project,** *22/5/2010)*

But simply put, modern science is saying that each of us is made up of the energy present 14 billion years ago at the origin of the universe.
>Since the so-called 'Big Bang' the universe

has been expanding and cooling ever since.
Every person is a mirror in which cosmic processes are reflected.
Every being is a 'pocket' of the universe.
Earth has birthed us.

> "For just as the Milky Way is the universe in the form of a galaxy, and an orchid is the universe in the form of a flower, we are the universe in the form of a human. And every time we are drawn to look up into the night sky and reflect on the awesome beauty of the universe, we are actually the universe reflecting on itself."
> *(Thomas Berry 2014)*

ooOoo

Bill McKibben claims it is time for radical change. It is urgent.
To recall the words of a long-haired, locust eating desert prophet:
    'The axe is at the root of the tree.'

Global warming is not just another important issue
that human beings need to deal with.
    Rather, it is the demand that we **live differently**.
    And it demands a paradigm shift in **who we think we are**.
    (McFague 2008:44)

On this I have also been reminded
that one of Judaism's main contributions to the human community
    is an 'ethics of restraint'.

> "In contrast to a life of out-of-control consumption, Judaism calls us as individuals to recognize that the earth and all of life is a gift from God – from that which creates the universe. It calls us to observe boundaries, to recognize our human limits and the limits of our planet. And Judaism calls us to restrain our desires so that all can benefit from the gifts of the earth and other human beings."

(Peters 2006:5)

So we do something important today.

To be reminded we are a part of nature,
> even as the oceans, the fauna, the storm and the cosmos, are…

A part of nature. A part of the universe. That whole

> "complex, interrelated and interacting... matter-energy in space-time... of which humans are an integral part…" *(Gillette 2006:1)*

Notes

Gillett, P. R. *"Theology Of, By, and For Religious Naturalism"* in **Journal of Liberal Religion 6**, 1, 2006, 1-6.

Hamilton, C. Scorcher: The Dirty Politics of Climate Change. Melbourne. Black Inc., 2007.

McFague, S. **A New Climate for Theology. God, the World, and Global Warming.** Minneapolis. Fortress Press, 2008.

McKibben, Bill. **Eaarth: Making a Life on a Tough New Planet.** Melbourne. Black Inc., 2010.

Peters, K. E. *"On the Frontier of Time"*. A Sermon. Unitarian Society of Hartford. 14 August 2006.

Peters, K. E. **Dancing with the Sacred. Evolution, Ecology, and God.** Harrisburg. Trinity Press International, 2002.

Tucker, M. E. & J. Grim. (eds). **Thomas Berry. Selected Writings on the Earth Community.** Maryknoll. Orbis Books, 2014.

THUNDER CAVE (a)

Come to a Place
Of danger and wonder
Overwhelming
In its horizoned immensities
Place always in the process
Of falling away from itself
Into the endless restlessness
Of all-receiving ocean

Ocean calling back to itself
These limestone shores
Of its own ancient downlaying
Reclaiming that
Which was its own wombing

Here i am captured
By these wave and wind intensities
On this sculptured-turmoil of coastland
Where maleable-stone
Unmitigating wind
And seething salt-water
Medumisticly entwine
In their anarchic alchemies

Yet --- today
There is but a modesty of ocean-edge
A modesty sharply-contrasted
By rock-craftings surreal and bizarre
Joining gouged-out cave-spaces
Above and around the edges
Of this ocean-churning
Here within this narrow-slot
Of sea-canyon

For here are iconic saga-stories
Of past and future maelstroms
Exponentially beyond
This present sea-experience
In its murmuring-growling potencies

These planet-empowered waters
Saturated with danger
And life-forming mysteries

Now to stand here mesmerised
In this compelling-moment
With near overwhelming compulsion
Enchanted to join on this serrated-edge
The song of age-long falling away
Allowing this liminal life
To be immersed again
In the harsh embrace
Of waves --- of rocks --- of undertow
Dissolved into this ocean
Of beserker-life
And mystery reformings (b)

John Cranmer
November 2017

(a)
A well-known place on Victoria's Great Ocean Road.
(b)
And one remembers the saga-stories of the transforming of life on the ocean beaches of deep time.

Theme focus: After Christmas/Year's end

14. AS WE LIVE IN THE UNSEEN G-O-D/CREATIVITY...

> "It may not be going too far to say that Christmas has always been an extremely difficult holiday to Christianize."
> *(Stephen Nissenbaum)*

In contrast to Matthew and Luke, who are the storytellers and scenario spinners charming us at Christmas with Lectionary stories about
> angels and shepherds,
> a birth in a stable,
> a villain named Herod,
> and heroes like the Magi...

the storyteller we call John plays the role of theologian.

After the Christmas curtain is raised...

> "In the beginning was the Word, and the Word was with God, and the Word was God. The Word was made flesh and lived among us"
> *(John 1:1)*

Well, theologian John certainly is, as he seeks to articulate his God-expressions. But, I for one, am still in holiday mood.
> The sand and sea water of the Central Coast
> are still between my toes!
> > And I'm not sure I am ready to be confronted
> > with this heavy theological treatise!

Yet neither do I want to just piously nod a slumbering holiday approval, for John's words bristle with possibilities
    that need to be appreciated. And examined.

ooOoo

In the G-o-d of John the theologian (or mystic if you follow Bishop John Shelby Spong) we repeatedly encounter a multi-moving, acting G-o-d.
    A 'verb' rather than a 'noun' is the way it is often described.

Which has encouraged Catholic feminist theologian Mary Daly to ask:

> "Why indeed must 'God' be a noun? Why not a verb - the most active and dynamic of all? ...The anthropomorphic symbols for God may be intended to convey personality, but they fail to convey that God is Be-ing."

And biblical scholar and founder of the Westar Institute/Jesus Seminar, Robert Funk, to suggest:

> "In Jesus' world, God is not an object, not even a person, whom one can observe here and there by keeping one's eyes open. When Jesus speaks about God, he is only observing his unseen God at work, he merely notes what God does. God himself or herself does not enter his field of vision. *(Funk 1994:106)*

Indeed, the new church season we are about to move into, called Epiphany, unveils and celebrates the presentness of this lively,
    innovative God, in everyday life.

Theologian John uses dynamic and relational words and images.
And in general terms so too does the whole of the biblical tradition:
> bringing, gathering, consoling, leading,
> understanding, granting, scattering,
> choosing, forgiving.

In these multiple actions, the god G-o-d is always 'acting'.
But I think we get a bit stuck when we hear the English translation, 'word'.
> In English, 'word' is usually given the meaning of
> sounds or its representation in letters
>> put together for oral or written communication.
>> Printed word.
>> Radio word.

But the Hebrew for 'word' is *'dabhar'* which means divine creative energy.
> The word that gave birth. Event.

Those of you who are right-brain thinkers will probably have already resonated with this and made a connection.
> For the Hebrew *'dabhar'* is about
>> the creative,
>> the imaginative,
>> the heart,
>> the feeling.

And this divine creative energy is more than just a concept.
The Season of Epiphany also reminds us that metaphorically the 'word' is made flesh.
> It lives among us.
> Moves within and among all things.
> Inspiring us to think and sing and dance
>> with integrity and historical and intellectual honesty.

As Lily Tomlin reminds us in her play *Search for Intelligent Life in the Universe...*
> We need to be aware of the goose-bump experiences of life.
> We need to practise 'awe-robics'.

ooOoo

The seasons we encounter
at this time of the Church year are several.
> Christmas.
> End of Year/New Year
> Epiphany.
> Summer holidays.

Sometimes it all seems one big mess!
No wonder we feel exhausted.

Popular culture and religion together.
All dating back hundreds of years...

The establishment of Christmas as a religious/christian festival first appeared on the liturgical calendar in Rome in 336 CE,
> and in the East in the late fourth century.

Prior to that, Epiphany (or 'old Christmas' celebrated on 6 January) was seen as more important than Nativity (celebrated on 25 December).
> The conflict was finally smoothed over with a decision
> > to combine Christmas with Epiphany, which liturgically
> > > became know as the 'Twelve Days of Christmas'.

There has always been a mix of folk-festival and religion around Christmas/Year's end.
So let me offer some comments by Mikhail Bakhtin when,
speaking of the cultures of the Renaissance and the Middle Ages,
> he said there always has been

"a boundless world of humorous forms and manifestations opposed [to] the official and serious tone of medieval ecclesiastical and feudal culture... Besides 'Easter laughter' there was also 'Christmas laughter'... expressed in gay songs. These songs of an extremely worldly content were heard in churches; some religious hymns were sung to worldly, even street tunes." *(Bakhtin 1984:4, 79)*

A closer examination of the pre-Christian folk-festivals shows they were essentially life-affirming. They said 'yes' to life.
    The Christianity of that time, essentially a religion of the monks, was pessimistic as regards this earth,
        and valued it only as a place of discipline for the life to come, which meant it was a religion
    of saying 'no' to the world.

In that situation, folk-festivals, and now popular culture, wins!

Life is not a great preparation for another place.
Neither is it a ready-made thing.
    Life is ourselves and what we make it.
    Life is a buzz that we generate around ourselves.
        It includes everything and excludes nothing. *(Cupitt 2003)*

Within Christian theology Christmas is the season
when we celebrate God-with-us Presentness.
    Traditionally this is called 'incarnation'.

John the theologian makes the incredible claim
that the one called Jesus/Yeshu'a of Nazareth is in the Presentness.

But 'incarnation' is more than just 'Christmas' or 'Christian' or even 'Jesus'. There is a wider spirit of incarnation, a more scientific natural 'doctrine of incarnation'…

> "that the universe itself is continually incarnating itself in microbes and maples, in humming birds and human beings, constantly inviting us to tease out the revelation contained in stars and atoms and every living thing."
> *(Bumbaugh 2003)*

The work of creativity, of incarnation, is not over
when the season of Christmas comes to an end.
> Incarnation is in the immensity of our evolving universe,
> > in the incredible display of evolving life-forms on this planet,
> > > and in the evolving society and daily living of the human species. *(Peters 2005:714)*

ooOoo

One year is ending and another commencing,
and in southern hemisphere Australian time we are actually in the midst of summer,
> when the sun beats down, the days are at their longest
> and the nights their shortest.

Light is something we have in abundance in December and January – we do not feel devoid of light when we celebrate Christmas or Epiphany – in fact,

> "especially when the glare of the scorching summer sun is at its harshest, we seek deliberately to escape from the light and retreat into the cool of the darkness for refreshment and relief."
> *(Johnson 2009:35)*

So let us celebrate the gift of our full humanity – in holiday time and festival time, and work together
for a more loving and caring communion
> with nature and with each other.

And along the way may we take time to pause...
for viewing pelicans in flight, and for smelling roses.
    Rarely do we experience the beauty of nature in depth.
        Instead we move on to something else,
           distracted just enough to miss that which is
        most important and immediate.

Notes

Bakhtin, M. **Rabelais and his World**. Trans. Helene Iswolsky. Bloomington. Indiana University Press, 1984.

Bumbaugh, D. *"Toward a Humanist Vocabulary of Reverence"*. Boulder International Humanist Institute, 22 February 2003.

Cupitt, D. **Life, Life.** Santa Rosa. Polebridge Press, 2003.

Funk, R. W. **Jesus as Precursor.** Revised edition. Sonoma. Polebridge Press, 1994.

Johnson, C. V. *"Relating Liturgical Time to 'Place-time': The Spatiotemporal Dislocation of the Liturgical Year in Australia"* in S. Burns & A. Monro. (eds). **Christian Worship in Australia. Inculturating the Liturgical Tradition.** Strathfield. St Paul's Publications, 2009.

Nissenbaum, S. **The Battle for Christmas. A Cultural History of America's Most Cherished Holiday.** New York. Vintage Books, 1996.

Peters, K. E. *"Confessions of a Practicing Naturalistic Theist"* in **Zygon 40,** 3, 701-720. 2005.

Theme: Cosmos

15. COMING HOME TO THE COSMOS...

> "Everything in the universe is related.
> Can you feel that umbilical cord to the Cosmos?
> Can you feel the strands of connectedness –
> the interdependent web – of all existence,
> even with all human beings?"
> *(M. DeWolf)*

Bruce Sanguin, the Canadian author and progressive minister in Vancouver, has written an important book called
Darwin, Divinity, and the Dance of the Cosmos.

It is from this book I have borrowed the title for this sermon.

Today, we celebrate the fourth Sunday in the new
Lectionary season called *Season of Creation.*
    And the theme for this day is Cosmos Sunday,
    hence the sermon title.

In the first chapter of his book, Bruce Sanguin tells of a time,
while still a theological student, he was in a café
    eating an egg salad sandwich and reading a poem.

The poem so affected him he said it felt as if

> "someone had peeled back a layer of reality to reveal the invisible radiance of what lay behind and within all creation."
> *(Sanguin 2007:20)*

So now that poem:
> This sunset...
> This smile...
> This word you are writing...
> This pain you are feeling...
> The question you are asking...
> This omelette you are cooking...
>
> The meaning of life
> is the tear of joy
> shed at the
> sight of the
> well-cooked omelette. *(J. Pramuk, in Sanguin 2007)*

Reflecting on his poem experience, Sanguin says:

> "If the poem I read expressed any truth at all, it was this: if we could truly see what is before our eyes, day in and day out, the sacred radiance of creation would drop us to our knees and render us speechless. We would know ourselves to be in as much divine presence as we can handle in this earthly realm." *(Sanguin 2007:21-22)*

Today, Cosmos Sunday, is an invitation once again to feel deeply and organically connected with planet Earth.

Today, Cosmos Sunday, is also an invitation for the Church to 'get with' a twenty-first century cosmological program...

> "There is a new story of creation, which needs to inform our biblical stories of creation... [And this new evolutionary cosmological story] simply cannot be contained by old models and images of God, and outmoded ways of being the church." *(Sanguin 2007:27-28)*

ooOoo

In every age, the worlds of theology and religion interact with the cultural and scientific world views of that day.

Such interaction between the two is essential

> "to make religious faith both credible and relevant within a particular generation's view of the world and how it works." *(Johnson 2007:286)*

Sharing Sanguin's concern, feminist Catholic theologian Elizabeth Johnson says:

> "In sum, theological reflection today should endeavor to speak about God's relation not to an ancient nor medieval nor Newtonian world, but to the dynamic, emergent, self-organizing universe that contemporary natural and biological sciences describe." *(Johnson 2007:287)*

Scientists tell us the 'Great Story' as we understand it today, begins with the ultimate mystery of the Big Bang, some 14 billion years ago.
>Life on Earth originated some 4.5+ billion years ago.
>*Homo habilis* (our ancestors) begin using tools 2.5 million years ago.
>Symbolic language emerges between 50,000 and 500,000 years ago.
>Classical religions emerge around 3,000-4,000 years ago.

Billions of years of cosmic evolution have produced us.
The ancestral stars are a part of our genealogy.
>"Out of the stars in their flight,
>>out of the dust of eternity, here have we come,
>>>Stardust and sunlight, mingling
>>>>through time and through space." *(Robert Weston 1993)*

If we put our 14 billion year universe on a clock of one hour,

> "humanity appears in only the last few seconds." *(Peters 2002:127)*

The sheer immensity of the cosmos/universe/planet
is very hard to get one's head around.

The fragments of knowledge we do have, suggest:
- one million bodies the size of Earth can fit in the volume of the Sun;
- each star has a sun;
- there are 100,000 million stars in the Milky Way galaxy;
- there are approximately 100,000 million galaxies;
- it has taken light 12,000 million years to reach us from the farthest reaches of space;
- the current diameter of the observable cosmos/universe is thought to be about 93 billion light years.

It is absolutely essential to make religious faith both credible and relevant within a particular generation's view of the world
and how it works!

ooOoo

In light of all this let me offer a couple of additional comments...
I invite you to ponder them sometime.

(i) Joel Primack (professor of physics) and Nancy Ellen Abrams (lawyer and writer) suggest the history of the universe is in every one of us.

> "Human beings are made of the rarest material in the universe: star-dust... Every particle in our bodies has a multibillion-year past, every cell and every bodily organ has a multimillion-year past, and many of our ways of thinking have multithousand-year pasts." *(Primack & Abrams 2006:89, 151)*

Likewise (ii) Karl Peters suggests that nature is in us as much as we are in nature.

> "We are webs of reality, woven out of the threads of culture, biology, and the cosmos according to recipes (structures of language and values, DNA codes, and laws of nature) in each. As webs of reality each of us is a manifestation of a large part of the universe as a whole." *(Peters 1992:412)*

Both these comments plus many others, go to the core of our beliefs: How can we now describe the experience we call G-o-d?

Traditionally it seems, most Christians have imagined the god G-o-d as The Creator, a kind of person-like reality
who has brought everything into being.

However all that is now changing.
New religious stories are being shaped. Stories which
> understand the presence of G-o-d that is compatible
> with the ideas of modern science.

And the new story, naturalistically conceived, is

> "as simply the creativity that has brought forth the world and all its contents, from the Big Bang all the way down to the present." *(Kaufman 2006:xi)*

Some of this thinking – called Religious Naturalism – was shaped by Harvard theologian, Gordon Kaufman. In his most recent and last book, Kaufman says:

> "Imagining God as creativity enables Christian thinkers to be much more attuned to what the modern sciences have been teaching us about our lives and the world in which we live. It makes it possible to bridge the divide often felt between religious faith and our scientific knowledge." *(Kaufman 2006:xi).*

So what does it mean to be progressively religious in the 21st century...? With help from others, some of my suggestions might include:
• To be progressively religious in the 21st century is to see ourselves "as webs of cosmos, life, and culture, so that we and the rest of our planet can continue and flourish." *(Peters 2002:136)...*
• To be progressively religious in the 21st century is to be devoted to maximising the future of the earth and all living creatures whose destiny is increasingly in our hands...
• To be progressively religious in the 21st century is to value the importance of the human relationships that bind us together into social groups...
• To be progressively religious in the 21st century is to place the needs of the global society before those of our own immediate family, tribe or nation. *(Geering 1998:46)...*
• To be progressively religious in the 21st century is to celebrate life.

Such a 21st century progressive religion is also, I want to suggest, a response to the vision and efforts and the life of
> the peasant Galilean sage we call Yeshu'a, without the baggage of christological beliefs unnecessarily added by the church. *(Wink 2000:177)*.

So where are we...
(i) If we put all this together the new Great Story suggests the whole universe is alive and changing, continually
> co-creating new possibilities of life.

Change **is!** Or remembering the ground-breaking work of Charles Darwin published nearly 160 years ago, **change** is the core of
> cosmic evolution,
> biological evolution,
> cultural/symbolic evolution. *(Peters 2002, Kaufman 2004)*

(ii) The word 'environment' literally means "that which surround us". So if we were actually to **notice** that which surround us, then following the comments of ethicist, Jack Hill,

> "At the very least, we would *notice* changes in the seasonal flights of birds. We would *notice* if the mosquito population doubled or tripled. We would *notice* if more and more trees had dead limbs. Instead of reading about the effects of global warming, we would *notice* them in our daily experience!" *(Hill 2008: 68)*

As contemporary progressive theology reminds us time and time again, G-o-d or the Sacred or Creativity does not reside in some other place called 'heaven'.
    Nor is heaven our goal.

The world is our true home. Indeed, our only home.

> "This life is meant to be enjoyed. To enjoy life is to cherish the beauty of each living thing, to be interested in diversity and difference in the web of life."
> *(Christ 2003:116).*

May the story told by the ones who discovered that the whole cosmos/universe/planet is alive and changing, continually, and
    that novelty and surprise makes life interesting
    always awaken within us new possibilities for the now.

Notes

Ayala, F. J. *"The Evolution of Life: An Overview"* in M. K. Cunningham. (eds) **God and Evolution. A Reader.** Oxon. Routledge, 2007.

Birch, L. C. Nature and God. London. SCM Press, 1965.

Christ, C. P. **She Who Changes. Re-imagining the Divine in the World.** New York. Palgrave Macmillan, 2003

DeWolf, M. L. *"What do we Mean – 'Thank God for Evolution'?"* Nature Coast Unitarian Universalists Church. The ClergyLetter Project web site, 2008.

Geering, L. **Does Society Need Religion?** Wellington. St Andrew's Trust for the Study of Religion and Society, 1998.

Hill, J. A. **Ethics in the Global Village. Moral Insights for the Post 9-11 USA.** Santa Rosa. Polebridge Press, 2008.

Johnson, E. A. *"Does God Play Dice? Divine Providence and Chance"* in M. K. Cunningham. (ed.) **God and Evolution. A Reader.** Oxon. Routledge, 2007.

Kaufman, G. D. **Jesus and Creativity.** Minneapolis. Augsburg Fortress, 2006.

– – – – –, **In the Beginning... Creativity.** Minneapolis. Fortress Press, 2004.

Peters, K. E. **Dancing with the Sacred. Evolution, Ecology, and God.** Harrisburg. Trinity International, 2002.

– – – – –, *"Interrelating Nature, Humanity, and the Work of God: Some Issues for Future Reflection"* in **Zygon: Journal of Religion & Science 27,** 4, 1992, 403-419.

Primack, J. R. & N. E. Abrams. **The View from the Centre of the Universe. Discovering our Extraordinary Place in the Cosmos.** New York. Riverhead Books, 2006

Sanguin, B. **Darwin, Divinity, and the Dance of the Cosmos. An Ecological Christianity.** Kelowna. CopperHouse/Wood Lake Publishing, 2007.

Weston, R. T. *"Out of the Stars"* in **Singing the Living Tradition.** Boston. Beacon Press/UUA, 1993.

Wink, W. *"The Son of Man the Stone that Builders Rejected"* in Jesus Seminar. **The Once and Future Jesus.** Santa Rosa. Polebridge Press, 2000.

PLANET AND SELF ENTWINED (a)

We who share the intimacy
Of cells atoms and particles
Always in dynamic reciprocation
Essence received and returned
Essence received and returned
i live nestled into your safekeeping
Always in dynamic communion
As a sacred interchange at the heart
Of ALL THAT IS

Through you i know *life*
Physical and aware
Without you i would be *nothing*

We continue to leap together
Out the Cosmic Womb that is *now*
Declared in that considered *big bang*
At beginning of our *all that is*
Continually actional within the intimacy
Of this particular cellular life!

You are the "me"
That will always be "me"
You are the "me"
That will never be "me"
Yet symbiotically always "me"

The intense mystery that confronts
As we explore what *is* and is *us*

We look with open-mouthed gaze
Into the wonder of our essential oneness
And our declaration of planetory community
Continually on multi-trajectories of Radical Becoming!!

John Cranmer
August 2017

(a) In conversation about the most appropriate feminine metaphor for the planet.

Theme focus: Family

16. CHALLENGING THE STATUS QUO AND INHUMANITIES...

> "...our life is no more than a bundle of stories, mostly half-finished... nevertheless, our life still matters, fragmentary and fictitious though it is."
> *(Don Cupitt)*

For the past ten years or so, I have been engaging with my families stories. And all seem to have strong connections with Scotland, Ireland and England.

With just a touch of Italy and Malta on my father's side, thrown in for good measure.

Yep, I am one of the 14 million or so people to sign into the global website *ancestry.com* to search out their familial past!

When researching the Dickson/Lampard mob - my mother's side, I made a couple of interesting discoveries:

(i) the family can trace its tree back to a Richard Keith, son of Harvey de Keith, Earl Marshall of Scotland in the early 1400s - hence the surname Dickson;

(ii) a James Dickson, sixth child of James Dickson, grandson of James Dickson, great grandson of James Dickson (I think there's a pattern developing here!),

was born on 5 August 1807, and later was to become the Tollkeeper of the Lamberton Toll House in Mornington, Berwick-on-Tweed.

So when our son was born, we followed tradition.
We called him Brendan!

James, the Tollkeeper of the Lamberton Toll House in Mornington, Berwick-on-Tweed. So I did what many others do...
> I checked out *Wikipedia* to see what I could find out about the Toll House.
> Apart from collecting road taxes and protecting some royal 'dalliances', I also read:

> "The now demolished Old Toll House at Lamberton, situated just across the border in Scotland [on the Great North Road], was notorious for its irregular marriages. From 1798 to 1858 keepers of the Toll, as well as questionable men-of-the-cloth used to marry [run-away] couples..."

The researcher of the family history, I guess taken aback by this discovery, added these comments:

> "The public associated these marriage houses with images of irate fathers chasing errant daughters and their boyfriends determined to elope... [but] records show the majority of couples to have lived within 30 miles... Roughly a third were Scots."

All of this tickled my fancy!
And I wondered why this was never spoken about at family gatherings.
> Making such personal 'untold' discoveries about one's families can be such fun!
> Even when Grannie doesn't think so!

oo0oo

Jesus of Nazareth was a Palestinian (Galilean) Jew. He was not a
Christian. He never rejected his Jewish 'family tree' roots.
> His spoken language was a Galilean dialect of Aramaic,
>> an identifiable accent and manner of speech
>> disdained by the religious elite and urban dwellers.

Indeed, more than that. One only needed to come from Galilee
or be in a group of Galileans to arouse suspicion and cause trouble!
> The dialect could prove to be deadly. *(Horsfield 2015:14)*

The society he and his family were born into was diverse
and highly stratified socially, economically and religiously.
> Boundaries were all the go.

And they all lived under the broken bodies and crushed spirits of
> compulsory offerings to the Jerusalem Temple,
> taxes to Herodian landlords, and
> tribute to their Roman conquerors.

The sum total of taxes levied upon the people, including religious
obligations, was nothing short of enormous.
> A tiny percentage of wealthy and powerful families
> lived comfortably in the cities from the tithes, taxes, tribute,
> and interest they exacted from the vast majority of people,
>> who lived in villages and worked the land.

As several scholars have recorded, the purpose of taxation was not
social well-being but enhancement of the position of elites. Period.
> Leadership was concerned with plundering
> rather than with developing! *(Herzog 1994:180)*

Named among those who were despised and hated
because of their abusive behaviour against the poor
were representatives of the Temple
> as well as toll collectors.

Jews regarded toll collectors as collaborators who profited
by preying on the country people on behalf of the Roman Empire.

The storyteller we call Luke even has a story about them.
Actually there are two stories about them.
> (i) The Jesus story. Short. Sharp. Leaving little other than questions.
> (ii) The Luke adaptation of that Jesus story some fifty years after the original.
>> And his conclusion: Pharisees are smug, self-seeking, judgmental.

We heard the latter as the Gospel reading. *(Luke 18:9-14)*
Traditionally...
(i) that story has been called the parable of the Pharisee and the Tax Collector,
> due to an incorrect translation of the word *'telones'*...
> It should be Toll Collector...

> "normally Jews who had become tax-farmers for the Romans - or in Galilee for Herod Antipas." *(Funk 2002:50)*

Traditionally...
(ii) that story has been read as a contrast between two types of oppositional piety:
> the arrogant and the humble...

Traditionally...
(iii) that story has been interpreted by some as a story about prayer: being persistent and humble...

All these traditional readings of the parable are, I suggest, unfortunate misnomers.
All these traditional readings either 'spiritualise' the story, or make it an example story,

rather than hearing the raw, blunt edge of the situation.
All these traditional readings are full of literary traps for unwary readers and listeners!

ooOoo

There is something both *sad* and *radical* about this particular Lukan Jesus story. I wonder if you heard either/both?

The *sad* bits...
The **Pharisee**, a member from the faction of moral entrepreneurs and rule-creation, stood apart.
> He did not want to risk contacting uncleanness
> from brushing the garment of an 'earth-worker' - those who failed to observe
>> the rules of purity laws.
>
> His 'standing apart', it seems, was to emphasise his self-importance, his prominence, and his power over others.

The **Toll Collector's** 'standing apart' from the congregation was because "he was a deviant shunned by the faithful." *(Herzog 1994:185)*
> He was hated. He didn't belong. And he knew it!
> He sought to be inconspicuous.

And the *radical* bits...
A Toll Collector (hear 'sinner') in the Temple grounds was unheard of! And the hearers of this story - so-called fellow sinners - would
> have drawn that conclusion before the story's end.
>> Both he and they were excluded, despised,
>> ruled and taxed over.

So what have we...
The actions of the Toll Collector were outside the negative prescribed script of others.

But he refused to accept the labels and limitations imposed on him by the religious pure.
> He never rebuts the Pharisee's shaming nor his efforts
> to reinforce the status quo, instead

"[he] speaks directly to God, seeking mercy. He breaks through the intimidation and fear that the Pharisee's words [prayer] have created, and by his actions, challenges the Pharisee's reading of God's judgments… He claims God's ear for himself".
(Herzog 1994:192)

That's right! G-o-d listening and speaking outside official channels! A 'sinner' at the Temple praying, seeking: Include me in!
> Make an atonement for me!
>> How radical can you get?

This radical…
- Jesus had a positive regard for toll collectors and all who were outside the social and religious boundaries of others;
- all brokered religion *(that is, priestly mediators are the necessary link between G-o-d and the individual)* is at an end. G-o-d's domain has no brokers.

And even more radical…

"A brokered religion produces a cyclical understanding of the faithful life: sin, guilt, forgiveness - the latter at the hands of the church and priest… In addition, it tends to produce a passive relation to the Christian life… [a] passivity carried over into the social, economic, and political realms as well."*(Funk 2002:131)*

No wonder Jesus' <u>*Galilean family*</u> and friends, always under suspicion because they were Galilean,
thought of him as a threat to their welfare.

Even mentally unstable!
No wonder Jesus' *hearers then,* heard a voice that shattered settled reality and opened up some new possibilities!
And when the muted ones began to speak,
>   their speech was funded by

> "the burdens of rage, alienation, resentment, and guilt. These burdens had been reduced to silence, but now they are mobilised in their full power and energy." *(Brueggemann 1989:51)*

No wonder Jesus' *hearers now,* who consider brokered Christianity (hear 'orthodoxy') and the evangelical 'prosperity gospel' simply incredible, are shunned and considered outsiders, even heretics!
>   And just in case you missed it: a non-brokered Christianity goes against nearly everything Church Christianity has structured and theologically claimed,
>> since the early fourth century!

oo0oo

The early followers of Jesus did not make claims about him because they sensed in him a different essence,
>   or saw a halo circling his head!

They made claims about him because they had heard him say and seen him do certain things. They experienced him acting in their lives.
>   And what they experienced in the company of this person, empowered and moved them deeply. *(Patterson 1998:53)*

The life to which he called his followers involved a *reversal* of ordinary social and political, cultural - and too often - religious standards.

These words of Canadian Bruce Sanguin ring true:

"Jesus was proclaiming the end of one era for humanity and the dawning of a new one - one person at a time... [His] very being was a proclamation of what the new human looked like... In his teachings he conveyed new spiritual wisdom, which if adhered to, effectively overturned the world of conventional wisdom."
(Sanguin 2015)

If Jesus is continued to be remembered,
it will no longer be because people give him divine titles...
> He will be remembered as long as his words offer an abiding challenge. *(Dewey 2015:4)*
> The radical challenge of distributive justice.
> The empowering challenge to move forward from the ugly inhumanities
>> "in which we seem to be trapped toward reconciliation of contending peoples,
>> nations, cultures, [and] religions." *(Kaufman 2006:113)*

Luke's Jesus misses all this.
So too does the spiritualised Jesus of traditional or 'orthodox' interpretations.
> One example should suffice.

In his challenging book ***The Wisdom of Jesus,*** professor of religious studies, Charles Hedrick, writes:

> "The early church's message to the world was strikingly different from what Jesus had said. Whereas Jesus proclaimed the sovereign rule of God, the church proclaimed Jesus – specifically the church proclaims salvation through his crucifixion and resurrection. And this proclamation became known as the gospel – 'the good news.' Calling it 'good news' obscured the fact the language of the gospel is steeped in religious institutionalism..." *(Hedrick 2014:34)*

But we can rescue Jesus from the cloying baggage of christological beliefs unnecessarily added by the church.

I invite you to accept the challenge to ponder some more credible alternatives.
> Both about the human sage called Jesus.
> And about those we or our church or government exclude for political reasons.

As the former outspoken advocate for the environment,
Thomas Berry, has lamented:

> "To learn how to live graciously together would make us worthy of this unique beautiful blue planet that was prepared for us over some billions of years, a planet that we should give over to our children with the assurance that this great community of the living will nourish them, guide them, heal them and rejoice in them as it has nourished, guided, healed, and rejoiced in ourselves."
> *(Berry 2014: 190)*

Notes

Berry, T. *"Spirituality and Ecology: A Sermon"* in M. E Tucker & J. Grim (eds). **Thomas Berry: Selected Writings on the Earth Community.** New York. Orbis Books, 2014

Brueggemann, W. **Finally Comes the Poet. Daring Speech for Proclamation.** Minneapolis. Fortress Press, 1989.

Cupitt, D. **What is a Story?** London. SCM Press, 1991

Dewey, A. *"Editorial: Testing the Atmosphere of God"* in **The Fourth R 28,** 1, 4. 2015.

Funk, R. W. **A Credible Jesus. Fragments of a Vision.** Santa Rosa. Polebridge Press, 2002.

Hedrick, C. W. **The Wisdom of Jesus. Between the Sages of Israel and the Apostles of the Church.** Eugene. Cascade Books, 2014.

Herzog 11, W. R. **Parables as Subversive Speech. Jesus as Pedagogue of the Oppressed.** Louisville. Westminster/John Knox Press, 1994.

Horsfield, P. **From Jesus to the Internet. A History of Christianity and Media.** New York. Wiley-Blackwell, 2015.

Kaufman, G. D. **Jesus and Creativity.** Minneapolis. Fortress Press, 2006.

Patterson, S. **The God of Jesus. The Historical Jesus and the Search for Meaning.** Harrisburg. Trinity Press, 1998.

Sanguin, B. **The Way of the Wind: The Path and Practice of Evolutionary Christian Mysticism.** Kelowna. CopperHouse/Wood Lake Publishing, 2015.

Theme focus: Land/Power

17. AN INDIGENOUS GIFT: LIVING WITH THE LAND...

> "Your desert, whose ever-shifting sands reflect the
> constant changing in our own lives,
> Whose dry heat brings interludes of repose,
> Show us the beauty that comes with purity
> and teach us how to simplify our lives."
> *(Tom Rhodes)*

Some time ago, the well respected journal *New Internationalist* published an article on the state of the global environment.
    In part that article said:

> "Human activity is putting such strain on the natural functions of the earth that the ability of the planet's ecosystems to sustain future generations can no longer be taken for granted. The provision of food, fresh water, energy and materials to a growing population has come at considerable cost to the complex system of plants, animals and biological processes that make the planet habitable."
> *(NI, No. 378, May 2005)*

Such warnings were and are not new.
And they continue to be debated - endlessly!
    But do we really see and heed these warnings?
    Or do they just massage us, washing over us,
        because we feel too powerless to go beyond simple acts?

ooOoo

Today is Land Sunday. A time to reflect on the land
    on which we walk, live, grow things,
        plough and mine, are usually buried in,
            and unfortunately, often pollute.
Or to use some short-hand language: 'real estate'.

But some scholars tell us that this understanding stands in sharp contrast to the biblical tradition. They assert there are at least four characteristics of land in the biblical tradition:
    (i) as mother of life,
    (ii) as abundant sustainer of living beings,
    (iii) as altar for worship of the Creator; and
    (iv) as home place. *(Ched Myers 2011:83)*

Earth is our author and no character can defy the pen of the creator! We live in a dynamic universe.

In recent years, we in Australia have also been made aware
of a different understanding of land/earth.
    An awareness that comes from
        the indigenous Aboriginal peoples.

As in the past, Aboriginal clans today hold deep religious links with their lands which were formed in the Dreaming.

The land belongs to the Aborigines and the Aborigines to the land. As an explanation of their myths instructs us:

> "The great ancestral creative beings, who journeyed across the continent at the beginning of time, established the land boundaries between different Aboriginal groups and the sacred sites. Carrying out ritual obligations at these sacred sites and performing religious ceremonies are the way by which Aborigines feel bound to their lands and protective towards it." *(Hill 1993).*

Aboriginal people do not live on the land.
> They live with the land.
> They are bound to it by spiritual links.
> They are 'earth dreaming' people.

Australian academic David Tacey suggests the main language in Australia is earth language.

> "The sacred songs and chants [of Aboriginal peoples] are sung to gigantic and ancient rock formations and to vast expanses of red earth. The sacred dances are earth dances, where the celebrants gather to 'sing up' and sustain the spirits of the earth. Significantly, Aboriginal dance and celebration is concentrated upon the movements of the feet." *(Tacey 2000:96)*

We now know Aboriginal people
have lived in Australia and the Torres Strait Islands
> for more than 60,000 years – perhaps even longer.

We now estimate that at the time of the arrival of the First Fleet in 1788 there was between 500,000 and a million Aboriginal people in the land.
And we also know that the policy of *terra nullius,*
or 'empty land belonging to no one',
> which took effect from the moment Captain Arthur Phillip arrived in 1788, has severely devastated the Aboriginal peoples and their traditional lands.

In 1992, the High Court of Australia, in its now famous Mabo decision, rejected the doctrine of *terra nullius*
as part of Australian law.
> Justice William Deane, later to become Australia's Governor General, said that

> > The doctrine of *terra nullius*... provided the legal basis for the dispossession of the Aboriginal peoples of most of

their traditional lands. The acts and events by which that dispossession in legal theory was carried into practical effect constitute the darkest aspect of the history of this nation. The nation as a whole must remain diminished unless and until there is an acknowledgement of, and retreat from, those past injustices... The lands of this continent were not *terra nullius*.

Strong, passionate words from one who is known universally
as being very compassionate!

There is still much we should know and do and work towards.
Aboriginal peoples in the main remain disenfranchised – powerless –
> because of prevailing attitudes and the exercise of power, others – governments and people – have over 'the land' and our history.

On a Sunday when the theme is 'Land'
thoughts on reconciliation between Aboriginal
and non-Aboriginal peoples
> need to be pondered some more, and
>> continuing dialogue and even compensation, encouraged.

The Revd Dr Djiniyini Gondarra from Galiwin'ku (Northern Territory, Australia), in some wise words, says:

"We, the Aboriginal people, are a gift to the land and to the people who come here. You who have come these last 200 years are also a gift to us. Justice, honesty and genuine reconciliation is the result when we have respect and honour for one another."
(Gondarra 1988:6)

ooOoo

Perhaps there is just an echo of some of this
in Matthew's Lectionary story *(Matthew 18:23-34)*
>in the difficult story/parable of the 'Unforgiving slave'.

The echo of power, especially 'power over'...
But we will not hear this echo if we spiritualise it.

The 'slave' or high-ranking bureaucrat
has power over other subordinates.
He is responsible for collecting tribute from them,
>as they are from others.
>>And he has done this very well, using calculating
>>and cunning tactics.

Likewise the bureaucrat's 'ruler' or master,
in a pure display of unfettered power,
threatens to totally destroy him
>because he has overreached himself
>and can't pay what is immediately due the master.

This scenario is then played out a second time.
But between the bureaucrat and one of his subordinates.
>Having been shamed before the master
>he must gain some prestige by exerting power
>over a subordinate.

That's our story.
To put it in context, the hearers of the story
would have been poor rural Galileans.
While both debts were large, with one much larger than the other
>both involve sums of money that most rural villages would
>never see. *(Herzog 1994:143)*

There are several twists or surprises in this story.
The first 'twist' comes when the master,
>in quite an extraordinary act for any agrarian ruler,

waives a debt of unimaginable proportions.
A second 'twist' comes when the bureaucrat, in a similar situation, does not act as his master does
>and therefore brings shame on his master
>>who now must act to save face.

For all the strength shown in the master's earlier decision,
the 'system', which supports all of them, is unable to show mercy.
>So the 'system', says the parable,
>>is not the place to look for a hopeful solution.

Which, I guess, is a different interpretation than that usually offered this parable!
However, another 'twist' reflected in the story
is the storyteller himself and the story's openness.
>Let me broaden this out a bit.

Loyal Rue, professor of philosophy and religion at Luther College, Iowa, in his book ***Religion Is Not About God,*** contends that religion
>is not about God but about us.

He argues that successful religions are narrative or myth traditions that influence human nature so we might
think, feel, and act in ways
>that are good for us,
>>both individually and collectively.
Rue writes:

> "Religious traditions work like the bow of a violin, playing upon the strings of human nature to produce harmonious relations between individuals and their social and physical environments. Religions have always been about this business of adaptation, and they will always remain so." *(Rue 2006:1)*

Now back to our story.
The final 'twist' is that the storyteller doesn't invite the hearer to

take sides. To blame someone.
> Instead, the storyteller seems to have Jesus/Yeshu'a
> drawing his hearers into wrestling with something
>> larger than the economic inequalities.

Something that might cause them to think, feel, and act in ways
> that are good for them,
> both individually and collectively.

So maybe a way into the parable is not via the sums of money,
> but the clash of values, specifically,
> of honour and shame.

> "The extreme penalty at the end indicates that the servant has violated something sacred..." *(Herzog 1994:146)*

In our situation, we may be willing to 'bash' the Banks
and their aggressive push for profits at the expense of borrowers.
> But are we also able to recognise how we so often live off
> the poverty of Asian 'sweatshops' and cheap labour
>> for our mobile phones, clothes, and house-hold items?

ooOoo

Most Australian Aboriginal leaders feel a powerful political 'system' does not fill them with hope in the matter of 'land rights'
> and the sacredness of the land.

Until recently – the last 45+ years or so – Aboriginal communities have had neither the resources nor access to the judicial process,
> to assert their land claims in the courts.

Because, as we heard echoed in Matthew's story about 'power over', justice questions come from below, not from above.
> They are raised by communities and individuals and clans
> who do not have social power or a voice
>> within the social or political system.

If the matter of 'land' is to be resolved in Australia,
then the solution will not come from a legal decision,
> but from political will,
>> and initiated by the people – you and me.

Saying 'Sorry' was certainly the hardest word of all to say
for at least one Australian government prior to 2007.
> It upset their perceptions of power – both political and economic.

But grace given and received is the only basis for reconciliation as we saw and experienced when a new/different post-2007 government did say 'Sorry'.
> Justice, honesty and genuine reconciliation
>> is the result when we have respect and honour
>>> for one another and for the land.

A comment in a recent post from *Charter of Compassion*
is suggestive as to what is required:

> "Let us reimagine the world we truly want to live in – not that which we simply wish to resist – and act as One Human Family with everything in our power toward that great vision!"

Maybe in all honesty we just need to ponder
all these stories a bit more…

Notes

Gondarra, D. **Father, You Gave Us The Dreaming.** Darwin. Published privately, 1988.

Herzog 11, W. R. **Parables as Subversive Speech. Jesus as Pedagogue of the Oppressed.** Louisville. Westminster/John Knox Press, 1994.

Hill, M. **Australian Aboriginal Culture.** Canberra. AGPS, 1993.

Myers, C. *"Land Sunday. Year A"* in N. C. Habel, D. Rhodes, & H. P. Santmire. (eds) The Season of Creation. **A Preaching Commentary.** Minneapolis. Fortress Press, 2011.

Rhodes, T. *"You Desert..."* in Roberts, E. & E. Amidon. (eds). **Life Prayers from Around the World. 365 Prayers, Blessings, and Affirmations to Celebrate the Human Journey.** New York. HarperCollins, 1996.

Rue, L. **Religion Is Not About God. How Spiritual Traditions Nurture our Biological Nature, and What to Expect when they Fail.** New Brunswick. Rutgers University Press, 2006.

Tacey, D. **ReEnchantment: The New Australian Spirituality.** Pymble. HarperCollins, 2000

LOST MANTRAS FOR GONDWANA

(1)
Walking the beaches
Out of Africa
Towards the sunrise
Open Horizons

(2)
Come and find this place   *Narrow seas due to*
This is sacred place   *lower sea levels than today*
Come cross narrow seas
Shining with the dawn

(3)
Come and recognise   *Plate Techtonics*
What collides and parts
Deep times ongoing
Tectonic dancing

(4)
Dream this virgin place
Deep tropic forest
A savage drying
Arid change to come

(5)
Ancient rivers flow   *Parts of the Finke River possibly*
Now in flood and drought   *400 million years ago*
Now desert fastness
What is still to come?

(6)
Pangia breaks   *Supercontinent broke up about*
Laurasia drifts   *200 million years ago*
Gondwana finds place
And now falls apart

(7)
Come look for a sea   *Eromanga Sea*
At the ancient heart   *110 million years ago*
Come find a known place
Of deep mystery

(8)
Remember sadness
Strong partnering loss   *Completed 30 million years*
Deep south land beyond   *Antarctica*
Ice-beauty still to come

(9)
Come ancient nations   *Objectively dated at least 60,000*
These ongoing waves   *years ago; some would say 80,000*
Finding their country
Dancing dream stories

(10)
Find the Dreaming Trails
Nations linked life shared
Stories sung lives danced
Agelong synergy

(11)
Ice-bound arid lands   *Last Glacial age in Australia*
Tell their recent tale   *Started about 25,000 years ago*
Emerge from cold thrall   *Ended about 12,000 years ago*
The sun comes again

(12)
The inflow of sea
Drowning the homelands
Isolating clans
Now the invader

(13)
See tall ships come
Nations fall away
Seek beneath our feet
Their remembered lives

(14)
Mighty continents
Know gradual return
This part-Gondwana
Back to Laurasia   *At least another 100 million years*

John Cranmer
April 2017

Theme focus: Creation/Universe

18. IMMERSED IN THE MYSTERIES OF 'CREATION'...

> "I am at home in the universe. I carry my home with me.
> No matter where I go, I cannot be less than at home...
> This world is our home, the home that is given us,
> the only home we know."
> *(Kenneth Paton (composite)*

Today we are returning to a venture we helped launch
several years ago.
The reshaping of part of the Revised Common Lectionary
    by adding to it a new season... 'Season of Creation',
        or in USA and other parts of the northern hemisphere,
        'Creation Time'.

Traditionally, the church calendar or Lectionary is shaped around
three years. And each year has seven main seasons:
    Advent, Christmas, Epiphany,
    Easter, Pentecost, Lent.
And the rather long general time, called After Pentecost
or Ordinary Sundays.

As I have said on several occasions,
this additional season claims some of that
After Pentecost time by designating the Sundays in September
traditionally associated with Spring in the southern
hemisphere, as the 'Season of Creation'.

In its initial shaping each of the four Sundays was given a theme.
>Year A: Forest, Land, Wilderness/Outback and River;
>Year B: Planet Earth, Humanity, Sky, Mountain;
>Year C: Ocean, Fauna and Flora, Storm, Cosmos.

With the first Sunday in October designated as 'Blessing of the Animals'

Of recent years some optional themes have been added:
>Year A: Volcano, Earthquake/Tsunami, Flood, Bushfire;
>Year B: Climate, Solar, Atmosphere, Rainbow. *(Habel et al. 2011)*

Why do all this?
Well, we must have been living under a cabbage leaf
if we hadn't heard the current universal debates
>about the environment, the ecological crisis,
>and the way human beings are treating the Earth.

Planet Earth is in peril. All creation is suffering.
As you can imagine or already know,
several folk have put their concerns
>in books,
>during workshops,
>at politically rallies; and
>through the media.

One such person is author and former Roman Catholic priest, Paul Collins. In his book ***God's Earth,*** he writes:

> "The beauty of nature and the wilderness has become vitally important for the spirituality of many people. It is increasingly in the cathedral of the environment that our contemporaries are rediscovering a way into the realm of the transcendent; they are discovering the sacred presence that stands behind the natural world." *(Collins 1995:226)*

And then this warning:

> "There is only one non-negotiable, and that is we have only one world - this one - and it is here and nowhere else that we will find God. If we destroy the world, we destroy not only ourselves but the most important symbol of God that we have."

Similarly, David Suzuki, several years ago, in ***The Sacred Balance:***

> "Forty years ago 'environment' simply meant 'surroundings'. What a distance we have travelled. Humanity has never before faced such a threat: the collapse of the very elements that keep us alive." *(Suzuki 1997:6)*

And again:

> "Today we believe that life cannot arise spontaneously, that life can only come from life. But once, at the very beginning, the first organism from which we are all descended was sparked into being, full of a life force that has so far persisted tenaciously for close to 4 billion years."

So I reckon it is important stuff we are doing this morning.
Both celebrating our kinship with creation, with nature, with the environment and expressing our concern about creation's future.

oo0oo

That kinship is also heard in part of the oldest Judaeo-Christian myth of creation.
    All living things are our kin,
    living in a forest vibrant with life.

While we are generally used to the stories called 'parables', we are not so used to the stories called 'myths'.
    Indeed we usually misinterpret myths

>>> as stories that are pre-scientific, false
>>> or 'sophisticated lying',
>>> or about some underworld
>>> full of gods and goddesses.

This is to mistreat those stories.
A story is a myth if it 'sets up' a world or tradition for people to live in.
> To recognise that the story does certain work
> and evokes certain sorts of responses.

> "In sum, a myth is a story that establishes a world. It directs people's religious awe, gives a sense of the whence and whither of the cosmos, establishes a social order, and provides psychological space." *(Tilley 1985:46)*

Joseph Campbell also says myths help us put our minds in touch with the experience of being alive.
> In a truly wonderful comment, I reckon, Campbell says:

> "People say that what we're all seeking is a meaning for life. I don't think that's what we're really seeking. I think that what we're seeking is an experience of being alive, so that our life experiences on the purely physical place will have resonances within our own innermost being and reality, so that we actually feel the rapture of being alive. That's what it's all finally about, and that's what [myths] help us to find within ourselves." *(Campbell 1988:5)*

So the Genesis myths are not to be taken literally
as if they were history or science.
That's the falsehood being taught as Creationism
and Intelligent Design (ID).
> The Genesis myths are to be heard as stories offering clues
> to the spiritual potentialities of the human life in relationship.

There are libraries full of creation stories,
all reported by decades of anthropological
and mythological research,
> some believed literally, some taken symbolically,
> some of which contradict others...
>> Australian Aborigines: 'The First Sunrise and Sunset'
>> Iroquois Indians: 'The First Animals and Twin Gods'
>> People of Japan: 'From the Floating Bridge of Heaven'
>> People of Iceland: 'The First Three Things - Ice, Fire, and Salt'
>> People of China: 'Yang and Yin and the Dwarf P'an Ku'

"Without a meaningful, *believable* story that explains the world we actually live in," writes Joel Primack and Nancy Ellen Abrams,

> "people have no idea how to think about the big picture. And without a big picture, we are very small people. A human without a cosmology is like a pebble lying near the top of a great mountain, in contact with its little indentation in the dirt and the pebbles immediately surrounding it, but oblivious to its stupendous view." *(Primack & Abrams 2006:84)*

As I have said in another place... Nature and naturalism are for us today 'the main game' for any progressive spirituality.

If we think back over the past two centuries and recount the ways modern scientific knowledge has impacted our lives,
> what would top the list?

I would suggest the recognition that nature
is constitutive of who and what we are as human beings.
> Whether or not we believe that there is something more,
>> nature is so significant that all our beliefs must be reformulated
>>> so as to take nature into account.

The forest and the bush are ideal places
to feel immersed in the mysteries of creation.
> And the first Sunday in a 'down under' Spring
> is a good day to begin the celebration of the
> Season of Creation.

Because Spring calls us forward to a 'new' religious sensitivity.
Of the need to reconstruct a theology
> which requires humans to remember their kinship
> with creation.

The 'old time' religion was centred on the individual.
The 'new' religion needs to be centred in relationships and the environment.

> "When we approach nature through the conceptualizing mind, we see a forest as a commodity, a concept. We no longer see it for what it truly is, but for what we want to use it as. It is reduced. This is how it becomes possible for humans to destroy the planet without realizing what they are doing."
> *(Eckhart Tolle)*

ooOoo

The Middle Eastern itinerant peasant sage, Yeshu'a/Jesus,
attempted to model a new kind of community with his followers.
> And he did this by reimagining the present and relationships
> through story. Parable to be exact.

But for several reasons, some chose to turn away.
> His model was too demanding.
> > His model was saying one's actions should not just be seen
> > > in terms of the end only, but in terms of
> > > the whole network of effects.

They lacked the imagination to see beyond the individual,
> so their own needs,
> so their own sense of power, could be satisfied.

They couldn't see that by not reaching out to others
- both out of concern as well as out of respect for the value of the other person - they were stunting their own lives.

Those who turned away were people of small 'size'...
To live the 'new' humanity which Jesus modelled,
> requires us to become people of 'S-I-Z-E'.

When we do, we begin to live in hope and can share in
the dream and the journey started by the Galilean.
> Because the future can always be different from the past.
> Where there is life, there is hope.

Notes

Campbell, J. **The Power of Myth.** Conversations with Bill Moyers. New York. Doubleday/Bantam, 1988.
Collins, P. **God's Earth. Religion As if it Really Mattered.** Melbourne. HarperCollins, 1995.
Fahs, S. L. & D. T. Spoerl. **Beginnings: Earth, Sky, Life, Death.** Boston. Beacon Press, 1937.
Habel, N. C.; D. Rhodes, & H. P. Santmire. (eds) **The Season of Creation. A Preaching Commentary.** Minneapolis. Fortress Press, 2011.
Patton, K. L. "I am at Home..." in Roberts, E. & E. Amidon. **Life Prayers from Around the World. 365 Prayers, Blessings, and Affirmations to Celebrate the Human Journey.** New York. HarperCollins, 1996,
and "The World..." in Patton, K. L. **Services and Songs for the Celebration of Life.** Boston. Beacon Press, 1967.
Primack, J. R. & N. E. Abrams. **The View from the Centre of the Universe. Discovering our Extraordinary Place in the Cosmos.** New York. Riverhead Books, 2006.
Suzuki, D. & A. McConnell. **The Sacred Balance. Rediscovering Our Place in Nature.** Sydney. Allen & Unwin, 1997.
Tilley, T. W. **Story Theology.** Wilmington. Michael Glazier, 1985.

Theme focus: Children/Education

19. CHILDREN: THE GENESIS OF HOPE...

> "Wonder rises up when we become identified with our vast and
> infinitesimal context, and experience ourselves
> as expressions of the same processes
> we observe around us."
> *(Paul Fleischmann 2013)*

A woman living in the slum area of a large city
was asked by a news reporter what hope she has, living as she must.
    She points to her children: "They are my hope", she says.
(Alves 2011)

                  ooOoo

Today, we celebrate Education Sunday as part of Education Week.
Already we have heard several stories of their own experiences...
    from a student,
    a teacher,
    a former head master
    and an assistant principal.

And like many other grandparents, we attended
'Open Day' at our grand-daughter's school.
    Small cup-cakes were made for our morning tea.
    We were shown artwork plus given a tour of the library.
        And the principal gave an address on the future of education

Education is important: be it for adults or children.
So I want to add to those comments already made
> by offering a few suggestions I have discovered
>> as a parent and grandparent, and
>>> learned from others.

For there is also much we could learn from a closer observation of children.

ooOoo

A child explores the world with true wonder
long before she understands what the adults mean by 'holy'.

A child does not need to be told in solemn pious tones
'only God can make a tree' before discovering the God-given thrill
> of climbing it,
>> feeling its rough bark against her hands and face,
>> sensing the joy of a new experience.

Out of such experiences in the life of a child
comes a quickened sense of self-worth,
> which has important ramifications
> for all relationships with other persons.

Perhaps this is why the peasant sage called Jesus/Yeshu'a
was also so affirming of children.

So in the spirit of this celebration this morning
I want to invite you to come on a journey of re-imagination.

We have heard from the story of creation *(Genesis Chapter 1)*...
Remembering that story, let us now re-imagine it
> not as a mythical story of the creation of the world,
> but as a mythical story of the creation of children.

All with the help of Sophia Lyon Fahs, Edith Hunter, plus friends
named and unnamed, who know a lot more about education
than I do.

To them I express my thanks and gratitude.

ooOoo

In a beginning...
At the start of every life, an environment must be created favourable
to life. Otherwise a child's surroundings would have no form or
shape and would be empty and unoccupied.

- So we who know, must move over the face of such a world
  to prepare it for a living child.

And G-o-d said: 'Let there be light...'
All through their life, children will be faced with
a mixture of light and darkness.

The child comes from the darkness of the mother's body into the
world where the light hurts its eyes.
> But light is good for the baby
> and all children must have lots of it all their life.

- We must see to it that the lights are turned on
  so the child's life will not be lived in the shadows of a darkened
  world.

And G-o-d said: 'Let their be a dome...'
A child must have support when born,
just as the planets must be supported in the sky.

And even though a child's prenatal experience
in the mother is a water event,
> the actual birth sets the child upon the solid earth.

• This earth, its water and its atmosphere
will be the child's home as long as the child lives.
>   And it is here, on earth, that the child must learn to live
>   just as other forms of life
>> live on the earth and in the sea.

Because this earth is the only one we have.

And G-o-d said: 'Let the earth put forth vegetation...'
It is important a child be provided with a total environment
favourable to healthy development.
>   This means green grass, plants, trees,
>   and all kinds of fruit, for healthy nourishment.

A child's life cannot mature properly
where the world of rivers, lakes and bush lands
>   have been changed into
>>   asphalt and brick,
>>   polluted streams and
>>   poisoned foods.

• A total environment must be given every child
with nature's surroundings at their finest and best.

And G-o-d said: 'Let the waters bring forth swarms of living creatures...
Every child needs to know animals,
>   what their kind is, and put a name on each,
>   as though each were a person.

And the child will have a 'reverence for life' - life of all kinds
for this is a part of the world of nature
>   and part of their own nature.

• We will need to relearn so we can teach
that the reverence for life makes no distinction
> between more precious and less precious lives.

And G-o-d said: 'Let us make humankind in our image...
A person is not 'made' all at once but is 'grown' from a baby.

Each child is born with a creative potential
that can only become known
> as the child develops talents and abilities.

And while this earth and everything in it is the child's domain,
each child must see to it that the balance of nature is maintained;
> food is provided for all earth's people,
> and life be made better for all living creatures.

• We must see to it that all children are given this birthright
and this heritage -
to be able to live life fully, and
to develop their capabilities to the fullest,
> ever mindful of the responsibilities,
> since we all walk this earth - its future in our hands.

The early stages of life are seldom entirely outgrown.
Rather, they become the platforms on which further stages of development are built.
> They must be supplemented by overlays of new levels of
> information that will shape the patterns of life.

So what this day celebrates is indeed important work!

ooOoo

Let us count it a privilege to walk with our children
    and grandchildren,
        our nieces and nephews.

Let us offer to shape their beliefs.
But always allow our beliefs to be reshaped by them.

> "Your children are not your children.
> They are the sons and daughters of Life's longing for itself.
> They come through you but not from you,
>   and though they are with you
>   yet they belong not to you…"
> *(Gibran 1926/1969:20)*

The wise among us call that wisdom.
And let us enable our children to wonder…

> "We are collections of long-nurtured solutions that have worked. It took a long time and a lot of editing to make every one of our molecules. As offspring of such a long streak of inspiring successes, let's allow ourselves [and our children and grand children] just a brief, momentary, 'Yeaaaay!'
> *(Fleischman 2013:255)*

ooOoo

There is a beautiful poem I have discovered in one of the books
I brought back from England in 2005.
    Let me share it will you now,
        as it is a story to share with all children.

It is called: *"A Short But True Story of You"*.
    You are made of star-stuff.
    You are related to every other living thing on Earth.

    You breathe out a gas that gives life to plants,
    and plants breathe out a gas that gives life to you.

You are part of a wonderful web of life
on a planet spinning in space.
When you die, someday, the elements of your body
    will become a part of clouds and crystals,
    seas and new living things.

You can think and wonder, love and learn.
You have the gift of life. *(Anderson & Brotman 2004)*

Let us remember all children and commit ourselves to
    their growth and safety,
    their health and education,
    their uniqueness and
    their unfolding beauty.

Notes

Alves, R. **Tomorrow's Child: Imagination, Creativity, and the Rebirth of Culture.** Eugene. Wipf & Stock, 2011.
Anderson, L. & C. Brotman. **Kid's Book of Awesome Stuff.** Biddeford. Brotman Marsh-Field Curriculums, 2004.
Fleischman, P. R. Wonder: **When and Why the World Appears Radiant.** Amherst. Small Batch Books, 2013.
Gibran, K. **The Prophet.** London. Heinemann, 1926/1969.

WILL'S TADPOLE SANCTUARY

There's an almost-secret place
Close to Will's house
Just down the hill from Ferny Creek School

I've walked here many times
And never thought there could be
a place like this --- **SO CLOSE!!**
Nestled within its steep scarp-edge
Perched precariously
On this dramatic sweep of land

So come with us
Over this 30 metres of uneven paddock
Rugged with grass and weeds and flowering bits
Come find this much-loved place
Guarded by tree-ferns and the blackberry's sharp-talons

Come make acquaintance
With this easily-overlooked almost-puddle
Yet the sense of this small place is very deep
Strongly-magnetic in drawing you here

This almost-secret water
Seems to be the upwelling
Of a natural spring
Enhanced by the mounding
Of soil and half-buried bricks
Giving this place it's ponding-opportunity

Yes --- here is this almost-puddle
Where water-weed grows
And tadpoles swim with some security
Except during the invasions of small boys
And sometimes their sisters and cousins
Their boots and their buckets

Here is this place of secrets
Not just for tadpoles but for Will himself
And his ongoing projects
Of experimental-wonder

John Cranmer
August 2016

Theme focus: Meaning

20. A NOD AND A WINK, AND MAYBE 'LIFE-ENHANCING'...

> "Human beings need only two things to have a
> rich and full existence.
> Not two cars, not two credit cards, not even two lovers.
> Just this: first, each of us
> needs a sense of gratitude for the life we have; and second,
> we need a way to express it."
> *(Loyal Rue)*

I understand from my Year 8 High School days
that the French language has a very small number of words in comparison to English.
    The various subtleties of meaning come from body language.

The British, being generally more reserved in temperament,
need more words...
The French, being perhaps more demonstrative in temperament,
need fewer words...

One of the interesting things about Internet communication is
there are various sets of characters that are used to express,
    in shorthand, the spirit in which something is said.

So a full colon followed by a dash, followed by a closing bracket,
makes up a smiling face.
    The statement is meant to be funny not serious.

If the colon is replaced with a semicolon,
this denotes a 'wink' - whatever a wink denotes!

Or, if you wish, you can 'insert an emoji' to express your feelings!
> There is an Internet/smart phone way of making meaning:
>> the spirit in which something is 'said'.

ooOoo

The translation of the Bible and/or the Christian scriptures
is not just a matter of a substituting a word in English
for a word in Greek.
> There are interpretive and cultural differences
>> of both the texts and the translators which also colour
>>> the meanings given to the words used.

Let me illustrate this by mentioning the old chestnut: 'virgin birth'.
Neither the word nor the concept of 'virginity'
> appear in the **Hebrew** text of Isaiah
> that storyteller Matthew quotes
> to undergird his story of the birth of Jesus.

The understanding of virgin is present only in the **Greek** translation
of the Hebrew. Much ink and book-burning has occurred
> because some bishops and fundamentalist preachers
>> were not prepared to allow scholarship to correct printed
> **English** translations.

Likewise, the Bible is not a scientific textbook. Bishop Jack Spong writes:

> "Jesus could not have imagined such an idea as Albert Einstein's theory of relativity… Concepts commonplace today in the world of physics, subatomic physics, astrophysics, and cosmology would have drawn from Matthew, Mark, Luke, and John, to say nothing of the author of the Book of Genesis, nothing except blank stares of incredulity."
> *(Spong 1991:25)*

Yet I still get mail from people and organisations inviting me to
attend the latest film on (un)Intelligent Design,
or distribute their propaganda,
> or trying to get up my nose by claiming that the Bible
> is the inerrant and authoritative word of the god G-o-d
> for all time, infallible, and without error
>> in matters of faith and practice!

And that I am letting the side down
with all this wrong 'progressive' stuff!

Now part of the problem with the Bible is it is often called the **Holy** Bible.
Thus, many have been taught its contents – a message from the god G-o-d – is set in concrete. Untouchable. **The** spiritual resource.

And... if G-o-d is trying to get a message to me,
to us through this book,

> "then we had better sharpen up and pay attention."
> *(Vosper 2008:220)*

But it isn't a message book.
Neither is it 'untouchable' or holy.
It is a very human collection assembled over a 1,000+ years
or more.

Those who want to insist otherwise, are putting the Bible in jeopardy, and becoming, even if unwittingly,

> "accomplices in bringing about the death of the Christianity they so deeply love." *(Spong 1991:32).*

Now all this doesn't mean we shouldn't take the Bible seriously.
We should. And when we do take the Bible seriously,
> a question we need to bring to every story is:

> "What do you make of it? not What is the meaning of the story? **You** bring the meaning to it. It's not there without you reading it and getting something out of it. You are the context in which it will be figured out and lived, if it's worth it."
> *(Vosper 2008:222)*

ooOoo

I mention all this because this is the freedom storyteller Matthew has. He uses that freedom all the time.
    And certainly so in this particular story. *(Matthew 16:13-20)*

So let's have another think about it.
Jesus seldom if ever, talks about himself
or tells stories about himself.
    When we read of such instances,
        it is probably the early Jesus Movement,

> "having Jesus speak its convictions about him, rather than Jesus himself speaking." *(Funk 2002:5)*

The story scene is set.
And what a challenge Matthew's Jesus gives the followers called 'disciples'.
    What are **they** saying?
    What's the talk? Who do **people/others** say I am?
    Who do **you** say I am?

Simon, the bloke with the nickname of 'stony ground', immediately jumps in. At least Matthew the storyteller has Simon jumping in.

Why?
What is the importance Matthew has attached
to this supposed dialogue?
Let me offer this suggestion.

Matthew (*Matityahu* in Hebrew), a convert to belief in Yeshu'a/ Jesus as Messiah, has Simon Peter, one of the so-called 'heroes' for Matthew's community,
> offering an interpretation, saying that this person Jesus,
>> the new Moses, who spent his days seeking out and accepting
>>> the hospitality of 'saints' and 'sinners'...
>> that this person Yeshu'a/Jesus reflects G-o-d.

Not the Torah. Not the destroyed Jerusalem Temple. Not the Roman Empire. This Jewish person called Jesus as Messiah.

The story appears to be one of Matthew's attempts
to answer the question:
> who is this Jesus, for a group of 'reformed' Jews?

Traditional interpretation has it that this group are probably living in Antioch in Syria. But Australian biblical scholar Lorraine Parkinson suggests

> "there is good reason to place it within a Palestinian Jewish context... given Matthew's anti-Pharisaic standpoint... [and] Palestine, the home territory of the Pharisees."
> *(Parkinson 2015:122)*

ooOoo

So, what do you/we make of this story?
What is the meaning of the story for you?
> I invite you to ponder that question along with this story.

In the meantime, let me offer another's attempt
at giving it meaning...
Every time we recognise in someone else
> the presentness of G-o-d,
>> and they have a contribution to make to our lives,
>>> we ordain them to do so.

Every time we look askance at another,
and wonder what earthly use this person would be to society or ourselves, it is we who are the poorer -
> and, of course, ultimately the church and community as a whole suffers in the long run.

Perhaps this is why the storyteller's Jesus:

> "sternly ordered the disciples not to tell anyone he was the Christ".

That would be to point to a particular presentness of G-o-d
in just one individual.
But we will be blessed as we recognise and affirm
> the unique presentness of G-o-d in many individuals,
>> in all those around us.

Quiet apart from any scientific 'doctrine of incarnation',
as one person has described it, which suggests

> "that the universe itself is continually incarnating itself in microbes and maples, in humming birds and human beings, constantly inviting us to tease out the revelation contained in stars and atoms and every living thing."
> *(Bumbaugh 2003)*

> Such recognition is life-enhancing.

Notes

Bumbaugh, D. *"Toward a Humanist Vocabulary of Reverence"*. Boulder International Humanist Institute, 22 February 2003.

Funk, R. W. **A Credible Jesus. Fragments of a Vision.** Santa Rosa. Polebridge Press, 2002.

Parkinson, L. **Made on Earth: How Gospel Writers Created the Christ.** Richmond. Spectrum Publications, 2015.

Rue, L. *"Going Deeper: Spiritual Dimensions of the Epic of Evolution"* in Earthlight Magazine, 26, Summer 1997, pages: 12-13.

Spong, J. S. **Rescuing the Bible from Fundamentalism. A Bishop Rethinks the Meaning of Scripture.** New York. HarperSanFrancisco, 1991.

Vosper, G. **With or Without God. Why the Way we Live is More Important than What we Believe.** Canada, Toronto. HarperCollins, 2008.

Theme focus: Celebration/Life

21. THE CHALLENGE OF EXTRAVAGANCE AND CELEBRATION...

> "Sing to Life a new song!
> Sing to Life, all Creation!
> Sing of compassion and
> temper your deeds with kindness..."
> *(Rabbi Rami M. Shapiro)*

The anonymous storyteller and mystic called John
has told a very old story. *(John 12:1-8)*
    And this story seems to have been reworked several times
    as it appears in various guises in at least three other collections.

In John, it is a good woman.
In Luke, a sinful woman.
In Mark, the woman anoints Jesus' head.
In Luke and John, she anoints his feet.
    Later generations wrongly imagined the woman was Mary
    Magdalene, whom tradition describes as 'a sinner'.

And the differences go on.
    In John, Judas objects.
    In Matthew, the disciples object.
    In Mark, it was some of those present who object.
    In Luke, it was Simon the pharisee who objects.
    In Matthew and Mark, all this took place in the house of
    Simon, the leper.
    In Luke, it happened in the house of Simon, the pharisee.
    In John, it took place in the home of Lazarus.

Confused? Well... we certainly have quite a story!

ooOoo

Amid all the changes to this story,
I began to wonder: where is this story's focus?
Perhaps that will give us a clue to the meaning
the storyteller wants to share.
> So in response to my own question
> I make the following suggestion.
> The focus is on the response of the woman.

But, as we also know, the woman's response is not always welcomed.
The protests in many of these stories
> seem to focus on the waste of resources,
> > with those resources going to assist the poor.

So as a guide, biblical scholar William Loader offers this comment:

> "It is not that we should see [her response] as stroking the ego of Jesus, but rather as indicative of her response... A person is responding to love and acceptance. It is not the time to talk budgets, but to value the person."
> *(W. Loader Web site 2004)*

ooOoo

During the process of thinking and talking about this story,
I found myself remembering some other stories along the way.
> Stories such as:
> > The man who had two sons;
> > A man with a hundred sheep; and
> > A woman with ten coins.

So I went back to them and started to read them again, out loud.
And this is what I heard.

• In the parable of the man who had two sons
we meet the younger son who,
>   after collecting his share of the family's estate,
>   leaves home and spends it all on extravagant living.

When he returns home, broke, he is welcomed back by his father
>   who bankrolls an extravagant homecoming party.

• In the parable of the one sheep missing from a flock of a hundred,
the fellow goes off searching for the lost one until it is found.

And when he finds that one sheep, throws a party in an act of extravagance, and maybe even offering the sheep
as part of the party food!

• Likewise, in the parable of the woman who loses a coin.
With a sense of urgency, she lights a lamp,
>   sweeps the house, and goes searching.

And she doesn't give up until she has found that lost coin.
Then she throws an extravagant party, probably spending
>   that coin and several others, in honour of the recovered coin.

Extravagance and joy characterise these three Lukan stories.
As it does, I reckon, in the story told by John.
>   But what of John's added comment:
>   " There will always be poor around, but I won't always be around".

Well, again I decided to go back and 'hear' that again,
checking the passage from Deuteronomy
>   that many scholars feel John has been inspired by.

And this is what I heard:

"Since there will never cease to be some in need on the earth,
I therefore command you, 'Open your hand to the poor
and needy neighbour in your land'. " *(NRSV)*

Open your hand... Be compassionate to others!
  Com- passion. Feeling with.
  From the very depths of the person.
  From our guts!
    More than just nice thoughts and warm feelings.

So with the broader Deuteronomy text ringing in my ears,
I reckon this story from John implies that it was:
  Mary - with the lotion and the touch,
    whose response was genuinely compassionate, and not
  Judas - with the speech and the pious-sounding advice.

The speech by Judas sets up a competitive situation
and a closed hand. The action of Mary sets up common likenesses
and an open hand.

Matthew Fox of 'creation spirituality' fame, has some interesting comments on compassion that I feel could be helpful:

> "Competition isolates, separates and estranges. Compassion unites, makes one, and embraces... If we can move from competition to compassion we will have moved from dull and moralistic and ungrateful and legalistic [thinking]... to celebrative thanking... Celebration leads to fuller and fuller compassion."
> *(Fox 1979:72, 89)*

ooOoo

Extravagance and celebration and joy!
For of such are the images of the 'glimpsed alternative',
>> and 'revelation of potential' called the realm/kin-dom of G-o-d as suggested by the sage Yeshu'a/Jesus.

But perhaps there is a step before all that.
The challenge of extravagance and celebration commences
>> when we actually start to take note of life around us...
>> When we begin to notice what is wonderful and refreshing!

"We rarely take the time to appreciate our eyes..." suggests Vietnamese Buddhist philosopher Thich Nhat Hanh.

> "We only need to open our eyes, and we see every kind of form and color – the blue sky, the beautiful hills, the trees, the clouds, the rivers, the children, the butterflies."

And when we do take the time to follow Thich's suggestion, then maybe we too can tell a similar 'sunset' story...

> "I will never forget a sunset about twenty years ago... The sky was so vivid, the clouds so magnificent, that commuters pulled their cars over to take in the moment. I was with my husband, and a small crowd of people gathered where we were standing on a cliff at a park overlooking the ocean. As the sun set, this group of strangers received a gift of nature. Our fellow sun worshippers gasped and sighed, commenting to others in the improvised congregation about the vibrant shades of purple and orange, sharing a communal sense of amazement and gratitude. It was obvious that all who gathered felt a spiritual connection to creation in this dazzling act of communing."
> *(Butler Bass 2015: 254-55)*

When next you are enjoying a quiet summer's evening on your verandah and looking towards the west,
become conscious of the sun's position.

Honour the sunset with your complete attention.
And as it lights up the sky heralding the end of another day,
> light a candle as our ancestors did
> to feed the sun as it begins to turn toward darkness.

Enjoy and celebrate!
And when you arise the following morning, ponder in your heart:
> What will be possible when we learn to truly celebrate each other and the rest of the Earth?

Notes

Butler Bass, D. **Grounded: Finding God in the World. A Spiritual Revolution.** New York. HarperOne, 2015.

Fox, M. **A Spirituality Named Compassion and the Healing of the Global Village, Humpty Dumpty and Us.** Santa Fe. Bear & Company, 1979.

Hanh, Thich Nhat. **Essential Writings.** (ed.). Robert Ellsberg. Maryknoll. Orbis Books, 2001.

Scott, B. B. **Re-Imagine the World. An Introduction to the Parables of Jesus.** Santa Rosa. Polebridge Press, 2001.

– – – – -, Hear Then The Parable. A Commentary on the Parables of Jesus. Minneapolis. Fortress Press, 1989.

Shapiro, R. M. *"Sing to Life!"* in Roberts, E. & E. Amidon. (eds). **Life Prayers from Around the World. 365 Prayers, Blessings, and Affirmations to Celebrate the Human Journey.** New York. HarperCollins, 1996.

Theme focus: Evolution

22. OF EVOLUTION AND G-O-D, AND THE UNFOLDING INTERCONNECTEDNESS OF LIFE...

> "We are Earthlings. We have a special connection to our planet.
> Earth is our platform and its history is our local owner's manual.
> We are partial products of its approximately four billion
> year old conditions."
> *(Fleischman 2013:340)*

Today, in the progressive religious world,
is **Evolution Sunday/Weekend.** So to celebrate this,
I want to talk very personally about G-o-d.

And a clue to what shapes both my experience
and understanding of science and the god G-o-d, is reflected
in the theme words (see above) of this sermon.

ooOoo

Let me go back a bit...
One of the very first books I ever bought on theology,
I bought in 1965, and by mistake.
    It cost me nine shillings.
    Its author was a biologist and process theologian.
I still have it on my library shelves even though it is beginning
to fall to bits!

I was in Warrnambool (Victoria) on a university break when one of
my former bank clients *(I used to be a bank teller)*
had just opened a bookshop,
    so a few of us went to celebrate the opening with him.

The shop was divided into sections
so I explored the 'Religion' section.
Among the books, one caught my eye.
> *Nature of God* was its title.

I bought it. But when I got home, I discovered
it was not called *Nature of God* at all.
> But instead, **Nature and God.**

Nevertheless, the book and its author, L. Charles Birch,
Challis Professor of Biology at the University of Sydney,
> has been a valuable travelling companion with me
> on my personal theological journey these past 50+ years.

The very first sentence in Birch's book is:

> "The concept of God's operations in the universe as a series of fitful interventions from a supernatural sphere overlaying the natural is quite unacceptable to science."
> *(Birch 1965:7)*

While the third sentence said:

> "On the other hand, the traditional thinking of science, sometimes called mechanism, is quite unreconcilable with any reasoned Christian position."
> *(Birch 1965:7)*

Since reading Birch way back then, an interest in communication,
> regular eye tests, and the relationship between
> science and religion, has remained with me.

Which is why, on Evolution Sunday,
I want to speak personally about G-o-d.

ooOoo

'G-o-d' is a symbol or word known and used by nearly everyone
who speaks the English language.
> But it is also a word which has many uses and meanings
> attached to it.

The *Macquarie Dictionary* defines the word as:

> "the one Supreme Being, the creator and ruler of the universe."
> *(Macquarie Dictionary 1981:763)*

This way of speaking theologically is called 'classical theism'.
This 'G-o-d' is supernatural, interventionist, and
> nearly always couched in male anthropological (or human-
> like) language and images.

For many, this is still the way they think
when they hear the word 'G-o-d'.
But this way of thinking doesn't work for me.

So over the years, my thinking has, and continues, to change.
> (i) I came to think of the god G-o-d as the creative process or
> 'creativity', rather than a being who creates; and
> (ii) I tried, in the main, to use non-personal metaphors rather
> than personal ones.

The thoughts of many others have interacted with my own thinking,
including those positively influenced by the work of Charles Darwin
> and his 1859 publication, ***On the Origin of Species.***

In that book, Darwin suggested that the world/universe was:
> (i) unfinished and continuing;
> (ii) involved chance events and struggle; and
> (iii) natural selection took the place of

"design according to a preordained [divine] blueprint."
(Birch 1965:29)

Put another way:

"In the beginning was creativity and the creativity was with God, and the creativity was God. All things came into being through the mystery of creativity; apart from creativity nothing would have come into being."
(Kaufman 2004:ix)

Or yet another way:

cosmic evolution, biological evolution, cultural/symbolic evolution. *(Peters 2002, Kaufman 2004)*

ooOoo

Today, we have mentally constructed another universe,
different from the traditional model.
    Both in science and in religion.

In **science**, the most widely accepted modern estimate
of the Earth's age - that third rock out from the Sun -
    is approximately 4.5+ billion years. While the observable universe - that whole

"complex, interrelated and interacting... matter-energy in space-time... of which humans are an integral part..."
(Gillette 2006:1)

    is approximately 14 billion years old, all let loose during an event called the Big Bang.

Mmm. A misleading term really, in that there wasn't really
    an explosion, but an expansion.

So awesome is the energy of this inflation process, writes Primack and Abrams,

> "that the smallest possible amount of it, so small that it fell below eternity's minimum threshold and disappeared through the floor – that subminimal bit became our entire universe."
> *(Primack & Abrams 2006:204)*

Science has pushed back the borders of mystery (as 'not knowing') and expanded the known universe immeasurably.

And science is saying the universe must be regarded **as a whole;** it is of **intrinsic value**, and each part,
>   galaxy,
>   organism,
>   individual atom,

participates in that intrinsic value as each part or web, participates in this wonderful web of life...

> "The great diversity of life, its myriad forms, is the rearrangement of macromolecules due to history, conditions, adaptations, and selections in a four billion year old wave that can raise up atoms and photons into mother-love."
> *(Fleischman 2013:342)*

Heirs to this long process of creative transformation,
we stand on the frontier of time, created by nature evolving
>   and with the opportunity to advance or diminish this magnificent creation.

Such science is public and cumulative and open to anyone
who wishes to pick up a book and read.
>   And a couple of good books, I reckon worth reading, are:
>>   Paul R. Fleischman, ***Wonder: When and Why the World Appears Radiant,*** and
>>   Joel Primack & Nancy Ellen Abrams, ***The View from the***

Center of the Universe: Discovering Our Extraordinary Place in the Cosmos.

As the debate over science and climate change and evolution rages in various parts of the world, a major concern is
> the whole misunderstanding of the 'theory of evolution.'

A common definition of theory is as a guess, a mere conjecture.
But in contemporary science, theory is an intellectual construct
> that opens the way to increased knowledge.

As it has been pointed out, biology in particular has found that evolutionary theory is the best design to add to humanity's store of knowledge:
> cracking the genetic code being a prime example.

After all, gravity is only a theory, but no one doubts its truthfulness.

Turning to the world of **religion**...
The 'naturalistic' strand of theology shaped by former Harvard University theologian, Gordon Kaufman,
> presents G-o-d naturalistically conceived
> as non-personal 'serendipitous creativity'

"manifest throughout the cosmos instead of as a kind of cosmic person. We humans are deeply embedded in, and basically sustained by, this creative activity in and through the web of life on planet Earth."
(Kaufman 2004:58).

Kaufman clearly names the problem with
traditional religious or theist language and thinking.
> Likewise, his alternative thinking and language embraces
> both our scientific knowledge
> and the reality beyond the symbols of biblical faith.

Others to help develop and promote this stand of thinking include Ursula Goodenough, Jerome Stone, Karl Peters, Joanna Macy, and Loyal Rue.
> Together, in various ways, they adopt the title
> 'religious naturalism'...

Generally speaking, religious naturalism is a religious response to the natural world. It engenders an attitude of reverence,
an ethos of caring for all of nature,
> and a spirituality inspired by contemplation of nature.

It is a way for all of us to unify our feelings about Nature.
It does not require a belief in the god G-o-d although it may include belief in g-o-d naturalistically conceived.
> For many religious naturalists the intellectual component of religious life takes the form of insight rather than specific beliefs.

The 'naturalism' represented by current advocates is diverse.
Generally speaking, they can be grouped as:
> (i) those who think of g-o-d as the totality of the universe considered religiously;
> (ii) those who conceive of g-o-d as the creative process within the universe;
> (iii) those who think of g-o-d as the sum of human ideals; and
> (iv) those who see no need to use the concept or terminology of g-o-d yet can still be called religious.

Religious naturalists also recognise that we do not live in straight lines. We truly do exist in a web, a network, a maze...

> "When the relationality is mutually supportive, and not distorted, we truly can speak of 'mazing grace'."
> *(Larry Axel 1987)*

Thus, progressive religious thought calls each and every one of us to 'dance with', to live in harmony with, our world.

> Given a chance, the cosmic evolution story – or 'Great Story' – is too compelling, too beautiful, too edifying, and too liberating to fail in captivating the imagination of a vast majority of humankind...

Captivating the imagination and the reality... of pelicans!

> "Its great wings outstretched, the... pelican spirals in the thermal air. Scarcely a flicker of those magnificent wings is required for it to soar further and further aloft. Finally reaching an apogee of the spiral, it gently banks and slowly descends, only to be uplifted again in its circling flight... For me, at that moment, this pelican's flight is a compelling symbol of the numinous powers, presences, and wonders of the natural order to which we both miraculously belong."
> *(Donald Crosby 2015)*

Experiences such as these throw life into a new frame.
> They rend the veil of the ordinary.
> They interrupt and can sometimes transform one's life.

ooOoo

New technologies and theories are allowing us
to see a universe no one ever could have imagined.

For me and many others the evolutionary epic is a religious world view. We are on our immense journey, standing in a throbbing cosmos,
> the meaning of which we cannot comprehend,
> but the majesty of which we experience.
> *(Richard Gilbert 2009)*

We are made of the rarest material in the universe: stardust.
In the words of Connie Barlow,
> one half of the Dowd/Barlow 'Thank God for Evolution' team,

"Tell me a creation story more wondrous than that of a living cell forged from the residue of exploding stars. Tell me a story of transformation more magical than that of a fish hauling out onto land and becoming amphibian, or a reptile taking to the air and becoming bird, or a mammal slipping back into the sea and becoming whale. Surely this science-based culture of all cultures can find meaning and cause for celebration in its very own cosmic creation story."
(Quoted in Dowd 2009:142)

Notes

Axel, L. E. *"Reshaping the Task of Theology"* in William Dean (ed.) *The Size of God. The Theology of Bernard Loomer in Context*, in **American Journal of Theology & Philosophy 8,** 1 & 2, January & May 1987.

Birch, L. C. **Nature and God.** London. SCM Press, 1965.

Crosby, D. **More than Discourse: Symbolic Expressions of Naturalistic Faith.** New York. SUNY Press, 2015.

Dowd, M. **Thank God for Evolution. How the Marriage of Science and Religion will Transform your Life and our World.** New York. Plume, 2009.

Fleischman, P. R. **Wonder: When and Why the World Appears Radiant.** Amherst. Small Batch Books, 2013.

Gilbert, R. *"And on the Eighth Day: Charles Darwin's Intelligent Design, Evolution, and our Faith"*. A Sermon. UU Fellowship of St. Croix, VI – February 15 2009.

Gillett, P. R. *"Theology Of, By, and For Religious Naturalism"* in **Journal of Liberal Religion 6,** 1, 2006, 1-6.

Kaufman, G. D. **In the Beginning… Creativity.** Minneapolis. Fortress Press, 2004.

Macquarie Dictionary. McMahons Point. Macquarie University, 1981.

Peters, K. E. **Dancing with the Sacred. Evolution, Ecology, and God.** Harrisburg. Trinity International, 2002.

– – – – -, *"Humanity in Nature: Conserving Yet Creating"* in **Zygon 24,** 4, 469-485.

Primack, J. R. & N. E. Abrams. **The View from the Centre of the Universe. Discovering our Extraordinary Place in the Cosmos.** New York. Riverhead Books, 2006.

Theme focus: Food/Eating

23. SLOW FOOD NOT FAST FOOD: WE ARE WHAT WE EAT...

"Once upon a time, somewhere far back in ancient human history
- so far back that personal survival was the only concern -
a defining event must have taken place.
Someone didn't eat what he found when he found it,
but decided to take it back to the cave to share with others.
There must have been a first time. A first act of community
- call it communion -
in the most elemental form."
(Fulghum 1995:79)

I really enjoy Robert Fulghum's writings.
And one of his books, **From Beginning to End** (above quote),
    is certainly a rewarding and imaginative read.

And it is from this book, along with some comments
from Brazilian Rubem Alves,
that I want to share some parallel thoughts
    to the Lectionary's shockingly graphic gospel story. *(John 6:51-58)*

The story from Fulghum's book...

ooOoo

Fulham tells of the time when his first son was in kindergarten, he was a parent volunteer who visited the school once a week
    to teach folk songs to the children.
    Singing came between rest-time and snack-time.

And he was regularly invited to stay after singing
and join the class for milk and scones.
"I gladly stayed. Not because I was particularly hungry, but because I enjoyed watching the children carry out this ordinary task with such extraordinary care."

He went on to describe how the children
set the table with serviettes and cups.
And arranged the chairs.

> "Others went to the refrigerator for cartons of milk, while two more fetched the scones from the kitchen and arranged them neatly on plates. One child was responsible for placing something in the middle of the table to talk about during the snack - a sort of 'show and tell'.

> "For half the class, their job for the day was being good 'guests'. The other half were the 'hosts'.

> "Each 'host' took a scone off the plate, broke it in half, and gave it to a 'guest' before eating the other half. During this snack-time, they discussed the 'show and tell' object in the centre of the table.

> "It was a high-point of my week. For me, it was communion."

Fulghum then goes on to add some other comments.

> "The sacraments are often defined by the church as 'outward and visible signs of an inward and spiritual grace'. Scones and milk with those children became a sacrament for me. Grace was clearly present. It was a ritual reminder that civilisation depends on sharing resources in a just and humane fashion."

ooOoo

Yeshu'a/Jesus is often represented as talking about food.
As he moved from place to place, the various storytellers
declared he would seek rest in a house.
>   Rumour has it once there he would make his way
>   to the cooking space
>   because there he knew he could find food
>   to transform his weariness into new energy and purpose.

For it is the cooking space - the kitchen -
that is the place of transformations, suggests Rubem Alves.

> "Nothing is allowed to remain the same. Things come in raw, as nature produced them. And they go out different, according to the demands of pleasure."
> *(Alves 1990:79)*

The raw must cease to exist for something different to appear.

> "The hard must be softened. Smells and tastes which were dormant inside are forced to come out: cooking is a magic kiss which wakes up sleeping pleasures... Everything is a new creature. Everything is made anew."

Jesus, so our tradition goes, often talked about food.
Slow food rather than fast food, that is.

And the gospel storytellers often put words in the mouth of Jesus
to have him speak about food and eating.
>   Bread and wine.
>   Body and blood.

But Jesus was no literalist.
And religious language is primarily metaphorical or poetic.
>   In other words, Jesus spoke so words would be eaten.

When bread and wine are eaten, they become body and blood.
When body and blood are eaten, they become compassionate deeds.
When compassionate deeds are eaten,
> they become as the sacred in our neighbour.

"We are what we eat," suggests Rubem Alves.

"One eats and one's body is resurrected." *(Alves 1990:86)*

Robert Fulghum suggests milk and scones
at kinder snack-time is communion. Is grace enacted.

"Since the beginning of time," Fulghum writes again,

> "people who trust one another, care for one another, and are deeply connected to one another have shared food as a sign of and a reaffirmation of their relationship... Every time we hold hands and say a blessing before a meal, every time we lift a glass and say fine words to one another, every time we eat in peace and grace together, we have celebrated the covenants that bind us together."
> *(Fulghum 1995:81-82)*

ooOoo

Let me now try to hang all this together
with some critical biblical studies...
As such I invite your careful listening/reading.

From all that we now seem to know, and do not know,
about biblical culture and early Christianities,
> we can acknowledge that meals played an important role
> > in the communal life of the followers of Jesus.

They regularly ate together, even before they began
to conduct worship services.
And the complete meal tradition they followed

– primarily the **Greco-Roman banquet** –
was one they inherited and which brought

"a wide variety of both Christian and non-Christian concerns to expression."
(Smith & Taussig 2001:103)

Traditionally, the gospel story from John has been interpreted with strong sacrament overtones.
> Holy Communion or Eucharist overtones, that is.

If that does indeed reflect the case, then it very much reflects John's community many years after the life and times of Jesus.
> When things were getting organised, institutionalised, and rules – the do's and don'ts of life – were being put in place.

Now, while none of the New Testament texts provide a liturgical 'script', there are explicit instructions regarding the celebration of the so-called 'Eucharist'
> in a early document that didn't make the canonical cut.
>> It is commonly called the *Didache*.

And here's an important bit...
These instructions, in this mid-first century document, have
> no references to a Last Supper tradition,
> no mention of the death or resurrection of Jesus; and
> no words of Jesus interpreting the bread and cup in terms of his own death!

The meal celebrates life, not death.
And it is about **community formation and community solidarity.**

A blog post a couple of years ago on the Biblical Archaeology web site "Bible History Daily" caught my eye.

Written by Australian Andrew McGowan of Yale Divinity School, he suggested:

"Jesus was most clearly someone willing to eat with diverse company, less an inclusive host than an undiscriminating guest. Jesus appears as host only in quite different and more historically contentious material, relative to that where he is depicted as keeping bad company or being a wine-bibber. The 'guest' traditions about him are generally defensible; the 'host' traditions tend to be more influenced by later reflection than material that scholars in general would actually attribute to the historical Jesus.

Then McGowan continues:

"Nor should we forget the even more basic reality of physical need. Jesus was aparently an itinerant without direct means of support, and his willingness or even desire to be included indiscriminately is not really so surprising in itself. Hunger makes for interesting and diverse table fellowship."
(McGowan 2015)

Returning to Fulghum, whatever the sacrament of Holy Communion is, "it is an act that arises out of our humanity, not organized religion."
(Fulghum 1995:82)

ooOoo

May our common and shared humanity be experienced again this day as we celebrate community in the Banquet sacrament.
And may our celebration be a ritual reminder that,
as we share the bread and share the wine,
    civilisation depends on sharing resources
    in a just and humane fashion.

Notes

Alves, R. A. **The Poet, The Warrior, The Prophet.** Philadelphia. SCM/ Trinity Press International, 1990.
Fulghum, R. **From Beginning to End. The Rituals of Our Lives.** Oxford. Ivy Books, 1995.
McGowan, A. *"The Hungry Jesus"* on the Bible History Daily blog site: <www.biblicalarchaeo;ogy.org/daily/biblical-topics/bible-interpretation/the-hungry-jesus> (Accessed 21 March 2015).
Smith, D. E. & H. E. Taussig. **Many Tables: The Eucharist in the New Testament and Liturgy Today.** Eugene. Wipf & Stock, 2001.

And a personal PS

Some time ago our daughter was invited to a friend's place where each guest was to prepare their favourite dish (food) as the gift. Our daughter decided her gift would be to share her feelings of food and cooking in this personal story to her friend...

Food and cooking has been a major influence in my life, from child until now. My mother worked with food and preparation, so meals in my house were from all origins and always a feast.

As a child, my mother had us cooking in the kitchen, learning and creating – of course, back then we thought of it as a game, not knowing the importance until we were much older.

As a teenager growing up in Sydney, I learned very quickly that not everyone has the same 'Apple Pie' family. Every friend who walked through our doorway was greeted with home cooked smells – some they had never smelt before – and learnt that home-made Lasagne was a great afternoon snack.

When I moved out of home at 20, my mother gave me her *Woman's Weekly* recipe card box. Back in the 70s, she collected those tokens to get the complete set. It was important to her back then so I knew how important it was to pass onto me. It took me ten years, but I cooked every dish on those cards (except the odd scary meatloaf). It's funny, cooking for myself every night made me feel so independent.

My feelings on cooking have changed again. I now have a wonderful man [and son] to double my portions for.

My favourite past-time of all is throwing dinner parties. The food has to be exciting, for me too, and always different. I plan for weeks and can't wait to start the prep. Then I get to share it all with my friends as I watch them having a good time, knowing my little dishes of love have put them all in the same room as me.

So to add to your collection is a *Donna Hay* magazine. I've been collecting them for years. She is my favourite cook, as she has similar traits that I recognise – food symbolising comfort and love, and bonds of family... friends... lovers.

My wish for you is that you experience how important you make others feel through your cooking... the first lesson I learned from my mum.

POSTLUDE

My 'pelican' story – a very common occurrence on the NSW Central Coast where I now live – was told by philosopher and Unitarian religious naturalist, Donald Crosby. A similar experience of the ordinary is recounted by Brazilian Marcelo Gleiser.

Gleiser, a professor of natural philosophy and a professor of physics and astronomy, had just finished attending a conference in Durham UK and decided to take a walk around the city – with its magnificent castle and well-preserved eleventh-century Gothic cathedral – a true medieval jewel. He writes:

> "A public footpath meanders along the river. I approach it through a narrow alleyway just beneath the castle. A huge sycamore bowed ceremoniously over the dark green water. I paused to appreciate the view, infused with a deep sense of peace. A cloud of mayflies wobbled just above the current, joyfully celebrating their twenty-four-hour existence. Suddenly out of the depths, a salmon leaped some three feet into the air, swallowed one of them, and dived back with a noisy splash. The fish must have been at least six pounds, maybe more. I just stood there, motionless, mouth agape.
>
> "If there are such things as signs, this was one. Nature had just sent me a message; at least that's how I saw it, which is what matters. Few moments in my life had been more meaningful. A cozy warmth spread across my chest, as I experienced a kind of revelatory awakening. I had just witnessed the simple beauty of the unexpected. 'You need to get out into the wilderness more often. You're missing the magic,' said a voice in my head. This time, I was listening."
> *(Gleiser 2016:34-35)*

As I indicated in the Prologue... Whether the religious orientation gathered under the title 'religious naturalism' is called 'religion' or 'spirituality' or 'secular mysticism' I am not really too fussed. More of a concern for me is that progressive religious thought and 'natural' liturgy/ritual respond to the challenges framed by ecological scientists and religion scholars. And the key role of the place-time 'fit'.

Such a response, inspired by some thoughts of both Karl Peters and Gordon Kaufman, might be a kind of cosmic recipe for present 'season' and future 'self' formation:
- A recipe for dancing with and living in harmony with, our world and the various environments that help shape us;
- A call to live humanly and humanely;
- An invitation to hope. Not hope for any time other than this time. But hope for the fullest and the best that human beings together in concert can achieve.

In a time of ecological vulnerability and dislocation of the social fabric, contemporary religious naturalism's conceptions of and attitudes toward nature and religiosity have much to commend it. May this small collection of Addresses/Sermons and Poems be an invitation for others to continue the exploration.

COMBINED BIBLIOGRAPHY

Alves, R. *Tomorrow's Child: Imagination, Creativity, and the Rebirth of Culture.* Eugene. Wipf & Stock, 2011
— — — — —, *The Poet, The Warrior, The Prophet.* The Edward Cadbury Lectures. London. SCM Press/Trinity Press International, 1990
Anderson, H. & E. Foley. *Mighty Stories, Dangerous Rituals. Weaving Together the Human and the Divine.* San Francisco. Jossey-Bass Publishers, 1998
Anderson, L. & C. Brotman. **Kid's Book of Awesome Stuff.** Biddeford. Brotman Marsh-Field Curriculums, 2004
Aronson, R. *Living Without God. New Directions for Atheists, Agnostics, Secularists, and the Undecided.* Berkeley. Counterpoint, 2008
Axel, L. E. *"Reshaping the Task of Theology"* in William Dean. (ed). The Size of God. The Theology of Bernard Loomer in Context, published in *American Journal of Theology & Philosophy 8,* 1 & 2, January & May 1987
Axel, R. C. *"Meland and Loomer: Forging an Alternative to Patriarchal Secularism"* in W. C. Peden & L. E. Axel. (ed). *New Essays in Religious Naturalism.* Highlands Institute Series 2. Georgia. Mercer University Press, 1993
Babin, P. *The New Era in Religious Communication.* (Translated by David Smith). Minneapolis. Fortress Press, 1991
Bakhtin, M. **Rabelais and his World.** Trans. Helene Iswolsky. Bloomington. Indiana University Press, 1984
Barreto, S. *"Religious Naturalism Demystified: An Interview with Jerome Stone".* 2008. Published on the Religious Naturalism Association (RNA) web site: <www.religious-naturalist-association.org> (Accessed March 2017)
Barrett, J. E. *"Pragmatism, Process, and Courage"* in W. C. Peden & L. E. Axel. (ed). *New Essays in Religious Naturalism.* Highlands Institute Series 2. Georgia. Mercer University Press, 1993
Bausch, W. J. *A World of Stories for Preachers and Teachers.* Mystic. Twenty-Third Publications, 1998
Belletini, M. *"Mother's Day",* Sermon. First Unitarian Universalist Church of Columbus, Ohio. 13 May 2001. <firstcols.org> (Accessed August 2017)
— — — — -, *"Blessings at a Naming Ceremony for a Baby"* in Roberts, E. & E. Amidon. (ed). *Life Prayers from Around the World. 365 Prayers, Blessings, and Affirmations to Celebrate the Human Journey.* New York. HarperCollins, 1996
Berber, P. L. *The Heretical Imperative: Contemporary Possibilities of*

Religious Affirmation. New York. Doubleday, 1979

Berry, T. *"Evening Thoughts"* in M. E Tucker & J. Grim. (ed). **Thomas Berry: Selected Writings on the Earth Community.** New York: Orbis Books, 2014

– – – – –, *"Spirituality and Ecology: A Sermon"* in M. E Tucker & J. Grim (ed). **Thomas Berry: Selected Writings on the Earth Community.** New York. Orbis Books, 2014

– – – – -, *"The Dream of the Earth"* quoted in L. G. Geering. **The Greening of Christianity.** Wellington. St Andrew's Trust, 2005

Bode, B. A. *"Blessing of Animals"* Service. Hope Unitarian Church. 30 September 2001

Brueggemann, W. **Finally Comes the Poet. Daring Speech for Proclamation.** Minneapolis. Fortress Press, 1989

Bumbaugh, D. *"Toward a Humanist Vocabulary of Reverence".* Boulder International Humanist Institute, Fourth Annual Symposium, Boulder, Colorado. 22 February 2003. (Accessed 20 December 2015). <http://www.uua.org/sites/live-new.uua.org/files/documents/bumbaughdavid/humanist_reverence.pdf>

Butler, J. *"The Crash of the Can Market"* in **Eureka Street 19,** 3. 3 February 2009

Butler Bass, D. **Grounded: Finding God in the World. A Spiritual Revolution.** New York. HarperOne, 2015

Cairns, I. J. **Mark of a Non-realist. A Contemporary Reading of the Second Gospel.** Masterton. Fraser Books, 2004

Cook, H. T. *"Dust to Dust".* Harry T. Cook Essay. (29 September 2017) <revharrytcook@aol.com>

Coots, M. **Seasons of the Self.** Nashville. Abingdon, 1971

Cox, H. G. *"God's Last Laugh"* in **Christianity and Crisis,** (6 April 1987)

– – – – –, **The Feast of Fools. A Theological Essay on Festivity and Fantasy.** Cambridge. Harvard University Press, 1969

Craddock, F. **Overhearing the Gospel.** Nashville. Abingdon Press, 1978

Crosby, D. **More than Discourse: Symbolic Expressions of Naturalistic Faith.** New York. SUNY Press, 2015

Crossan, J. D. **God and Empire. Jesus Against Rome, Then and Now.** New York. HarperCollins, 2007

– – – – –, & J. L. Reed. **In Search of Paul. How Jesus's Apostle Opposed Rome's Empire with God's Kingdom.** New York. HarperSanFrancisco, 2004

Cupitt, D. **Above Us Only Sky. The Religion of Ordinary Life.** Santa Rosa. Polebridge Press, 2008

– – – – –, **Life, Life.** Santa Rosa. Polebridge Press, 2003

– – – – -, **Rethinking Religion.** Wellington, NZ. St. Andrew's Trust, 1992

– – – – –, **What is a Story?** London. SCM Press, 1991

Cusack, C. M. **The Sacred Tree: Ancient and Medieval Manifestations.**

Newcastle-upon-Tyne. Cambridge Scholars Press, 2011
Darwin, C. *On the Origin of Species by Means of Natural Selection.* London. Arcturus Publishing, 2008
Dewey, A. *"Editorial: Testing the Atmosphere of God"* in *The Fourth R 28,* 1, 4. 2015
Drees, W. B. *"Thick Naturalism: Comments on Zygon 2000"*, *Zygon: Journal of Religion and Science 35,* 4, (December 2000), 856
Fahs, S. L. & D. T. Spoerl. *Beginnings: Earth, Sky, Life, Death.* Boston. Beacon Press, 1937
Felten, D. M. & J. Procter-Murphy. *Living the Questions. The Wisdom of Progressive Christianity.* New York. HarperOne, 2012
Ferguson, T. W. & J. A. Tamburello. *"The Natural Environment as a Spiritual Resource: A Theory of Regional Variation in Religious Adherence"* in *Sociology of Religion 76,* 3, (2015), 295-314
Fleischman, P. R. *Wonder: When and Why the World Appears Radiant.* Amherst. Small Batch Books, 2013
Fox, M. *A Spirituality Named Compassion and the Healing of the Global Village, Humpty Dumpty and Us.* Santa Fe. Bear & Company, 1979
Fulghum, R. *From Beginning to End. The Rituals of Our Lives.* Oxford. Ivy Books, 1995
Funk, R. W. *Funk of Parables. Collected Essays.* Edited by B. Brandon Scott. Santa Rosa. Polebridge Press, 2006
– – – – -, "Editorial" in *The Fourth R 18,* 1, (2005), 2, 20
– – – – -, *A Credible Jesus. Fragments of a Vision.* Santa Rosa. Polebridge Press, 2002
– – – – -, *Jesus as Precursor.* Revised edition, edited by E. F. Beutner. Sonoma. Polebridge Press, 1994
Galston, D. Galston, D. *"Mysteria Poetica: Some Reflection of the God Question".* Westar Institute Ethics & Early Christianity Blog. 28 July 2017
– – – – -, *Embracing the Human Jesus. A Wisdom Path for Contemporary Christianity.* Salem. Polebridge Press, 2012
Geering, L. G. *Reimagining God. The Faith Journey of a Modern Heretic.* Salem. Polebridge Press, 2014
– – – – -, *From the Big Bang to God. An Awe-Inspiring Journey of Evolution.* Salem. Polebridge Press, 2013
– – – – -, *Coming Back to Earth. From gods, to God, to Gaia.* Salem. Polebridge Press, 2009
– – – – -, *The Greening of Christianity.* Wellington. St Andrew's Trust, 2005
Gibran, K. *Sand and Foam.* New York. Alfred A. Knopf, 1926/1954
– – – – -, *The Prophet.* London. Heinemann, 1926/1969
Gillette, P. R. *"Theology Of, By, & For Religious Naturalism"* in *The Journal of Liberal Religion 6,* 1, 2006

Gleiser, M. *The Simple Beauty of the Unexpected. A Natural Philosopher's Quest for Trout and the Meaning of Everything.* Lebanon. ForeEdge/ University Press of New England, 2016

Gondarra, D. *Father, You Gave Us The Dreaming.* Darwin. Published privately, 1988

Goodenough, U. *"Evolution is Not About Survival of the Fittest But About Fitting In"* A Sermon, preached at The First Unitarian Church of Alton. (No date). <www.firstuualton.org>

— — — — —, *"'Journey of the Universe': The Challenge of Telling Everybody's Story", 13.7 Cosmos & Culture:* Commentary on Science and Society web site, 31 March 2011 (Accessed April 2017)

— — — — —, *"Vertical and Horizontal Transcendence"* in **Zygon: Journal of Religion and Science 36,** 1, (March 2001)

— — — — —, *"Exploring Resources of Naturalism: Religiopoiesis"* in **Zygon: Journal of Religion and Science 35,** 3, (September 2000), 352 - 355

— — — — —, *The Sacred Depths of Nature.* New York. Oxford University Press, 1998

— — — — —, & P. Woodruff. *"Mindful Virtue, Mindful Reverence"* in **Zygon: Journal of Religion and Science 36,** 4, (December 2001)

Grigg, R. **Beyond the God Delusion. How Radical Theology Harmonizes Science and Religion.** Minneapolis. Fortress Press, 2008

Habel, N. C. **Rainbow of Mysteries: Meeting the Sacred in Nature.** Kelowna. CopperHouse/Wood Lake Publishing, 2012

— — — — —, **An Inconvenient Text: Is a Green Reading of the Bible Possible?** Hindmarsh. ATF Press, 2009

Hamilton, C. **Scorcher: The Dirty Politics of Climate Change.** Melbourne. Black Inc., 2007

Hardwick, C. D. & D. A. Crosby. **Pragmatism, Neo-Pragmatism, and Religion: Conversations with Richard Rorty.** New York. Peter Lang, 1997

Hedrick, C. W. *"The Church's Gospel and the Idiom of Jesus"* in **The Fourth R 30,** 4, July-August 2017, 3-7, 26

— — — — —, **The Wisdom of Jesus. Between the Sages of Israel and the Apostles of the Church.** Eugene. Cascade Books, 2014

— — — — —, **Parables as Poetic Fictions. The Creative Vice of Jesus.** Peabody. Hendrickson Publishers, 1994

Herzog 11, W. R. **Parables as Subversive Speech. Jesus as Pedagogue of the Oppressed.** Louisville. Westminster/John Knox Press, 1994

Hill, M. **Australian Aboriginal Culture.** Canberra. AGPS, 1993

Hocking, W. E. **The Meaning of God in Human Experience. A Philosophic Study of Religion.** New Haven. Yale University Press, 1912/1963

Hogue, M. S. *"Withdrawal from Paris Accord Reflects a 'Theopolitics' of American Exceptionalism"* in **Political Theology Today,** 29 June 2017. <www.politicaltheology.com> (Accessed August 2017)

– – – – -, *"Religion Without God: The Way of Religious Naturalism"* in **The Fourth R 27,** 3, (May-June 2014), 3-6, 15-16

– – – – -, **The Promise of Religious Naturalism.** Lanham. Rowman & Littlefield Publishers, 2010

Holloway, R. **Doubts and Loves. What is Left of Christianity.** Edinburgh. Canongate Books, 2001

Horsfield, P. **From Jesus to the Internet. A History of Christianity and Media.** New York. Wiley-Blackwell, 2015

Hunt, R. A. E. **When Progressives Gather Together: Liturgy, Lectionary, Landscape... And Other Explorations.** Northcote. Morning Star Publishing, 2016

– – – – -, & J. W. H. Smith. (ed). **Why Weren't We Told? A Handbook on Progressive Christianity.** Oregon. Polebridge Press, 2012

Hyers, C. *"The House of Laughter"* in **Presbyterian Survey 80,** 3, (April 1990), 29 - 31

Jenks, G. C. *"The Historical Jesus"* in R. A. E. Hunt & J. H. W. Smith (ed). **Why Weren't We Told? A Handbook on 'progressive' Christianity.** Salem Polebridge Press, 2013

Johnson, C. V. *"Relating Liturgical Time to 'Place-time': The Spatiotemporal Dislocation of the Liturgical Year in Australia"* in S. Burns & A. Monro. (ed). **Christian Worship in Australia. Inculturating the Liturgical Tradition.** Strathfield. St Paul's Publications, 2009

Karskens, G. D. **The Colony. A History of Early Sydney.** Crows Nest. Allen & Unwin, 2009

Kauffman, S. A. *"Breaking the Galilean Spell"* in **Edge,** (11 April 2008). <www.edge.org/conversation/stuart_a_kauffman-breaking-the-galilean-spell> (Accessed 20 October 2017)

– – – – -, "Beyond Reductionism: Reinventing the Sacred" in Edge, (12 November 2006). <www.edge.org/conversation/stuart_a_kauffman-beyond-reductionism-reinventing-the-sacred> (Accessed 20 October 2017)

Kaufman, G. D. **Jesus and Creativity.** Minneapolis. Fortress Press, 2006

– – – – -, **In the Beginning... Creativity.** Minneapolis. Fortress Press, 2004

– – – – -, **God-Mystery-Diversity. Christian Theology in a Pluralistic World.** Minneapolis. Fortress Press, 1996

Keen, S. **In the Absence of God. Dwelling in the Presence of the Sacred.** Edinburgh. Harmony Publishing, 2010

– – – – -, **Apology for Wonder.** New York. Harper & Row, 1969

Kirk, M. (ed). *"Worship Resource Material from the The General Assembly of Unitarian and Free Christian Churches, London, Recognising the 200th Anniversary of the Birth of Charles Darwin."* 2009

Kring, W. D. *"The Need for Humor".* A Sermon article. All Souls Church, New York City, (17 January 1971)

LaChapelle, M. D. *"Ritual is Essential. Seeing Ritual and Ceremony as Sophisticated Social and Spiritual Technology"* in **In Context**, 5, (Spring 1984), 39

Loomer, B. M. *"The Size of God"* in William Dean. (ed). The Size of God. The Theology of Bernard Loomer in Context, published in *American Journal of Theology & Philosophy 8,* 1 & 2, January & May 1987. (Also published in book form separately)

McDaniel, J. B. **Of God and Pelicans. A Theology of Reverence for Life.** Louisville. Westminster/John Knox Press, 1989

McEmrys, A. *"Living Liturgy: A Unitarian-Universalist Liturgical Theology in Theory and Practice"* in **The Journal of Liberal Religion 6,** 1, 2006

McFague, S. **A New Climate for Theology. God, the World, and Global Warming.** Minneapolis. Fortress Press, 2008

McGowan, A. *"The Hungry Jesus"* on the Bible History Daily blog site: <www.biblicalarchaeo;ogy.org/daily/biblical-topics/bible-interpretation/the-hungry-jesus> (Accessed 21 March 2015)

McKibben, B. **Eaarth: Making a Life on a Tough New Planet.** Melbourne. Black Inc., 2010

MacGillis, M. *"The Cosmic Walk".* A resource posted on <http://www.greenfaith.org/> (Accessed February 2017)

Martin, D. *"We are the Earth"* in Roberts, E. & E. Amidon. (ed). **Life Prayers from Around the World. 365 Prayers, Blessings, and Affirmations to Celebrate the Human Journey.** New York. HarperCollins, 1996

Matthews, C. **The Celtic Book of Days. A Celebration of Celtic Wisdom.** New Alresford. Godsfield Press, 1995

Mathews, F. Quoted in M. Dowd. **Thank God for Evolution. How the Marriage of Science and Religion will Transform your Life and our World.** New York. Plume/Penguin Group, 2007

Meland, B. E. **Modern Man's Worship: A Search for Reality in Religion.** New York. Harper & Brothers, 1934

Murray, S. E. *"Our Life has its Seasons"* No. 113 **Alleluia Aotearoa. Hymns and Songs for all Churches.** Raumati. New Zealand Hymnbook Trust, 1993

Myers, C. *"Land Sunday. Year A"* in N. C. Habel, D. Rhodes, & H. P. Santmire. (ed). **The Season of Creation. A Preaching Commentary.** Minneapolis. Fortress Press, 2011

Neu, D. L. **Return Blessings: Ecofeminist Liturgies Renewing the Earth.** Cleveland. Pilgrim Press, 2002

New York Times. *"Climate Change Report".* 8 August 2017. <https://www.nytimes.com/interactive/2017/08/07/climate/document-Draft-of-the-Climate-Science-Special-Report.html>

Nickerson, B. **Celebrate the Sun. A Heritage of Festivals Interpreted Through the Art of Children from Many Lands.** Philadelphia. J. B. Lippincott Co., 1969

Nissenbaum, S. **The Battle for Christmas. A Cultural History of America's Most Cherished Holiday.** New York. Vintage Books, 1996

O'Donohue, J. *Anam Cara. Spiritual Wisdom from the Celtic World.* London. Bantam Books, 1997

"Painting the Stars: Science, Religion and an Evolving Faith." DVD/Video. Produced by *Living the Questions,* 2013

Parkinson, L. *Made on Earth: How Gospel Writers Created the Christ.* Richmond. Spectrum Publications, 2015

Patterson, S. *The God of Jesus. The Historical Jesus and the Search for Meaning.* Harrisburg. Trinity Press, 1998

Peters, K. E. *"Wisdom in Ancient and Contemporary Naturalism".* A Presentation to 'Seizing an Alternative: Towards an Ecological Civilization' Conference, Claremont, 4-7 June 2015. <www.karlpeters.net> (Accessed 20 July 2017)

– – – – -, *"Toward an Evolutionary Christian Theology"* in **Zygon: Journal of Religion and Science 42,** 1, (March 2007), 49-63

– – – – -, *"On the Frontier of Time".* A Sermon. Unitarian Society of Hartford. 14 August 2006

– – – – -, *"Confessions of a Practicing Naturalistic Theist"* in **Zygon: Journal of Religion & Science 40,** 3, 701-720. 2005

– – – – -, ***Dancing with the Sacred: Evolution, Ecology, and God.*** Harrisburg. Trinity Press International, 2002

– – – – -, *"Storytellers and Scenario Spinners: Some Reflections on Religion and Science in light of a Pragmatic, Evolutionary Theory of Knowledge"* in **Zygon: Journal of Religion and Science 32,** 4, (December 1997), 465-489

– – – – -, *"Interrelating Nature, Humanity, and the Work of God: Some Issues for Future Reflection"* in **Zygon: Journal of Religion and Science 27,** 4, (December 1992), 403-419

– – – – -, *"Humanity in Nature: Conserving Yet Creating"* in **Zygon: Journal of Religion and Science 24,** 4, (December 1989), 469-485

– – – – -, *"Evolutionary Naturalism: Survival as a Value"* in **Zygon: Journal of Religion and Science 15,** 2, (June 1980), 213-222

– – – – -, *"The Image of God as a Model for Humanization"* in **Zygon: Journal of Religion and Science 9,** 2, (June 1974), 98-125

Phillips, S. *"Changing of the Seasons".* ABC News. **The Drum.** 21 March 2014. <abc.net.au>

Pilcher, C. *"Marking Liturgical Time in Australia: Pastoral Considerations"* in S. Burns & A. Monro. (ed). **Christian Worship in Australia. Inculturating the Liturgical Tradition.** Strathfield. St Paul's Publications, 2009

Preston, N. *"Eco-Theology: The Main Game for Religious Progressives"* in R. A. E. Hunt & G. C. Jenks. (ed). **Wisdom and Imagination: Religious Progressives and the Search for Meaning.** Northcote. Morning Star Publishing, 2014

– – – – -, *"Exploring Eco-Theology"* in R. A. E. Hunt & J. W. H. Smith. (ed). ***Why Weren't We Told? A Handbook on 'progressive' Christianity.*** Salem. Polebridge Press, 2013

Prewer, B. D. ***More Australian Psalms.*** Adelaide. OpenBook Publishers, 1996

Primack, J. R. & N. E. Abrams. ***The View from the Centre of the Universe. Discovering our Extraordinary Place in the Cosmos.*** New York. Riverhead Books, 2006

Ranson, D. *"Fire in Water. The Liturgical Cycle in the Experience of South East Australian Seasonal Patterns"* in ***Compass Theology Review*** 26, 1992. (Photocopy in private circulation)

Redd, N. T. *"Summer: The Warmest Season"*. ***Live Science***, 19 June 2015

"Religious Naturalism. A Religious Worldview Grounded in the Sciences, the Humanities, and the Arts". https://religiousnaturalism.org/what-is-religious-naturalism/ (Accessed August 2016)

Rhodes, T. *"You Desert..."* in Roberts, E. & E. Amidon. (ed). ***Life Prayers from Around the World. 365 Prayers, Blessings, and Affirmations to Celebrate the Human Journey.*** New York. HarperCollins, 1996

Rich, J. *"The Gifts of the Autumn Years"*. ***The Blog,*** 21 November 2011. <huffingtonpost.com>

Rue, L. ***Nature is Enough. Religious Naturalism and the Meaning of Life.*** New York. State University of New York Press, 2012. (Kindle Edition)

– – – – -, ***Religion Is Not About God. How Spiritual Traditions Nurture our Biological Nature, and What to Expect when they Fail.*** New Brunswick. Rutgers University Press, 2006

– – – – -, *"Going Deeper: Spiritual Dimensions of the Epic of Evolution"* in ***Earthlight Magazine***, 26, Summer 1997, pages: 12-13

Sanguin, B. ***The Way of the Wind: The Path and Practice of Evolutionary Christian Mysticism.*** Kelowna. CopperHouse/Wood Lake Publishing, 2015 (Pre-published copy)

– – – – -, ***The Advance of Love. Reading the Bible with an Evolutionary Heart.*** Vancouver. Evans & Sanguin Publishing, 2012

– – – – -, ***Darwin, Divinity, and the Dance of the Cosmos. An Ecological Christianity.*** Kelowna. Copper House/Wood Lake Publishing, 2007

Santmire, H. P. ***Nature Reborn: The Ecological and Cosmic Promise of Christian Theology,*** Minneapolis. AugsburgFortress Press, 2000

Scott, B. B. (ed). ***Jesus Reconsidered. Scholarship in the Public Eye.*** Santa Rosa. Polebridge Press, 2007

– – – – -, ***Re-Imagine the World. An Introduction to the Parables of Jesus.*** Santa Rosa. Polebridge Press, 2001

– – – – -, ***Hear Then The Parable. A Commentary on the Parables of Jesus.*** Minneapolis. Fortress Press, 1989

Shapiro, R. M. *"Sing to Life!"* in Roberts, E. & E. Amidon. (ed). **Life Prayers from Around the World. 365 Prayers, Blessings, and Affirmations to Celebrate the Human Journey.** New York. HarperCollins, 1996
Singing the Living Tradition. Boston: The Unitarian Universalist Association, 1993/2000
Smith, D. E. & H. E. Taussig. **Many Tables: The Eucharist in the New Testament and Liturgy Today.** Eugene. Wipf & Stock, 2001
Smith, E. J. *"Crafting and Singing Hymns in Australia"* in S. Burns & A. Monro. (ed). **Christian Worship in Australia. Inculturating the Liturgical Tradition.** Strathfield. St Paul's Publications, 2009
Spearritt, G. *"Religion: It's Natural!"*. (No date). Sea of Faith in Australia. <www.sof-in-australia.org/religion.htm> (Accessed December 2001)
Spong, J. S. **Liberating the Gospels. Reading the Bible with Jewish Eyes.** New York. HarperCollins, 1996
– – – – –, **Rescuing the Bible from Fundamentalism. A Bishop Rethinks the Meaning of Scripture.** New York. HarperSanFrancisco, 1991
(Staff Writer) *"Christianity: A Laughing Matter"* in **Insights. News/Magazine of the Uniting Church, NSW Synod.** (August 2002), 23-24
Stone, J. A. **Sacred Nature: The Environmental Potential of Religious Naturalism.** New York. Routledge, 2017
– – – – –, **Religious Naturalism Today. The Rebirth of a Forgotten Alternative.** New York. SUNY Press, 2008
– – – – –, *"Is God Emeritus? The Idea of God Among Religious Naturalists"* in **The Journal of Liberal Religion 5,** 1, 2005
– – – – –, *"Is Nature Enough? Yes"* in **Zygon: Journal of Religion and Science 38,** 4, (December 2003) 783-800
– – – – –, *"What is Religious Naturalism?"* in **The Journal of Liberal Religion 2,** 1, 2000
– – – – –, *"Inaugural Liberal Arts Lecture"*, 1998, William Harper College, Chicago, quoted in M. S Hogue. **The Promise of Religious Naturalism.** Lanham. Rowman & Littlefield Publishers, 2010
– – – – –, *"On Listening to Indigenous Peoples and Neo-pagans: Obstacles to Appropriating the Old Ways"* in C. D. Hardwick & D. A. Crosby. (ed). **Pragmatism, Neo-Pragmatism, and Religion: Conversations with Richard Rorty.** New York. Peter Lang, 1997
– – – – –, *"Bernard Meland on the New Formative Imagery of Our Time"* in **Zygon: Journal of Religion and Science 30,** 3, (September 1995), 435-449
– – – – –, *"Broadening Care, Discerning Worth: The Environmental Contributions of Minimalist Religious Naturalism"* in **Process Studies 22,** 4, (Winter 1993), 194-203
– – – – –, **The Minimalist Vision of Transcendence. A Naturalist Philosophy of Religion.** Albany: State University of New York Press, 1992

Swimme, B. T. & M. E. Tucker. ***Journey of the Universe.*** New Haven. Yale University Press, 2011

Tacey, D. ***ReEnchantment: The New Australian Spirituality.*** Pymble. HarperCollins, 2000

Tatum, W. B. *"John the Baptist and Jesus".* A Report of the Jesus Seminar. 1994. In private circulation

Taussig, H. ***A New Spiritual Home: Progresive Christianity at the Grass Roots.*** Santa Rosa. Polebridge Press, 2006

– – – – -, *"Ritual Theory Applied to 21st Century Christian Worship Practices".* A paper distributed to members of the Literacy & Liturgy Seminar, Westar Institute, 2006 (In private circulation)

Thich Nhat Hanh. ***Essential Writings.*** (Ed). Robert Ellsberg. Maryknoll. Orbis Books, 2001

– – – – -, *"Present Moment Wonderful Moment"* in E. Roberts & E. Amidon. ***Life Prayers from Around the World. 365 Prayers, Blessings, and Affirmations to Celebrate the Human Journey.*** New York. HarperCollins, 1996

– – – – -, *"Earth Brings us Life..."* in E. Roberts & E. Amidon. ***Earth Prayers from Around the World. 365 Prayers, Poems, and Invocations for Honoring the Earth.*** New York. HarperCollins, 1991

– – – – -, Various Sayings... (< https://www.brainyquote.com/quotes/authors/t/thich_nhat_hanh.html>) Plus material from the Wikipedia entry under his name. Accessed July and August 2017

Tucker, M. E. & J. Grim (Ed). ***Thomas Berry: Selected Writings On The Earth Community.*** Maryknoll. Orbis Books, 2014

Vogt, V. O. ***Modern Worship.*** Lowell Institute Lectures. New Haven. Yale University Press, 1927

– – – – -, ***Art and Religion.*** New Haven. Yale University Press, 1921. (Second printing 1929)

Vosper, G. ***We All Breathe. Poems and Prayers.*** Toronto. File 14: PostPurgical Resources, 2012

– – – – -, ***With or Without God. Why The Way We Live Is More Important Than What We Believe.*** Canada: Toronto. HarperCollins, 2008

Westerhoff, J. H. *"Contemporary Spirituality: Revelation, Myth and Ritual"* in G. Durka & J. Smith. (ed). ***Aesthetic Dimensions of Religious Education.*** New York. Paulist Press, 1979

White Jr, L. *"The Historical Roots of our Ecological Crisis"* in ***Science 155,*** 3767, (March 1967) <science.sciencemag.org>

Wink, W. *"The Son of Man the Stone that Builders Rejected"* in The Jesus Seminar. (ed). ***The Once and Future Jesus.*** Santa Rosa. Polebridge Press, 2000

Wood, N. *"You shall ask..."* in Roberts, E. & E. Amidon. (ed). **Life Prayers from Around the World. 365 Prayers, Blessings, and Affirmations to Celebrate the Human Journey.** New York. HarperCollins, 1996

Wright, C. *"We Are Stardust: Toward an Ecotheological Anthropology"* in **The Other Journal: An Intersection of Theology and Culture.** The Seattle School of Theology and Psychology. <theotherjournal.com> 28 August 2017. (Accessed 19 September 2017)

ABOUT THE AUTHOR

Rex A E Hunt *MSc(Hons), GradDip(Communication Management)*

Rex Hunt is a religious naturalist, progressive liturgist, and social ecologist. A retired minister of the Uniting Church in Australia, his last placement was at the progressive **Church of St James, Canberra**, ACT, having previously served in parish settings in Victoria, Tasmania, and New South Wales, spanning more than forty years.

In the middle of all this he was appointed **Director of Communications** with the National Assembly of the Uniting Church, serving in that position for nine years.

He was Founder and National co-ordinator of **The Network of Biblical Storytellers Australia/New Zealand** (1990-96), and Founding Director of **The Centre for Progressive Religious Thought, Canberra** (2002-09).

As part of his commitment to the progressive religion movements in Australia and New Zealand he was Chair of the Planning Team of **Common Dreams Conference of Religious Progressives, Australia/South Pacific** for eight years (2006-2013). He now serves as a member of the Committee of **Common Dreams Inc.** He is also a member of the **Religious Naturalist Association** and an Associate of the **Westar Institute**, where he served on its *Literacy & Liturgy Seminar*.

He and spouse Dylis live on the Central Coast of New South Wales (Australia). They have two married adult children: Brendan and Rowena, three grandchildren: Elsie, Romeo, and Lenna, and a grand-dog called 'Alfie'.

ABOUT THE POET

John Cranmer *BSocSci., MAppSci*

John Cranmer is a retired Uniting Church minister living in Melbourne's (Victoria) outer east, with spouse Marilyn.

As a poet, John looks to places of intense presence as the springboards for his poetry. These include the Murray River, the open horizons of the Nullabor, and the steep slopes of the Flinders and Dandenong Ranges.

Recently John, in co-operation with Denham Grierson, has produced a collection of poetic-pieces called **Walking on Bones.** The title offering a more than passing reference to Ezekiel's Vision of the Dry Bones.

He continues to be fascinated by the works of Carl Jung and the ongoing presence of the ancient spiritualities that arose with the coming to awareness of the human - sometimes called Shamanic.

www.ingramcontent.com/pod-product-compliance
Lightning Source LLC
Chambersburg PA
CBHW051939290426
44110CB00015B/2039